Bargaining
with
Uncertainty

BARGAINING WITH UNCERTAINTY

Decision-Making in
Public Health, Technological Safety,
and Environmental Quality

MERRIE G. KLAPP

AUBURN HOUSE
New York • Westport, Connecticut • London

Library of Congress Cataloging-in-Publication Data

Klapp, Merrie Gilbert.
    Bargaining with uncertainty : decision-making in public health,
technological safety, and environmental quality / Merrie G. Klapp.
        p.   cm.
    Includes bibliographical references and index.
    ISBN 0-86569-046-4 (alk. paper)
    1. Health risk assessment.   2. Medical policy.   3. Environmental
policy.   4. Uncertainty.   I. Title.
    RA427.3.K53   1992
    362.1'042—dc20   91–32712

British Library Cataloguing in Publication Data is available.

Library of Congress Catalog Card Number: 91–32712
ISBN: 0-86569-046-4

First published in 1992

Auburn House, 88 Post Road West, Westport, CT 06881
An imprint of Greenwood Publishing Group, Inc.

Printed in the United States of America

The paper used in this book complies with the
Permanent Paper Standard issued by the National
Information Standards Organization (Z39.48-1984).

10 9 8 7 6 5 4 3 2 1

Contents

Preface   ix

Chapter 1: Bargaining with Uncertainty   1

Bureaucratic Bargaining   2
Scientific Uncertainty as a Rationale   4
Alternative Case Studies   6
Outline of the Book   8
Appendix: The Primary Case Studies   9

Chapter 2: Uncertain Science   17

Statutory Requirements to Examine Science   18
  Environmental Policy: Federal versus State Mandates   19
  Food Additives versus Environmental Policies: Federal
    Mandates   20
Risk Assessment by Agency Scientists   21
  The Saccharin Case   21
  The Dioxin Case   24
  The LNG Case   27
Scientific Controversy   28
  Institutional Settings   29
  Roles of Scientists   30

Risks   32
Types of Scientific Uncertainty   32
Summary   42

Chapter 3: Bargains with Citizens   43
The LNG Case   45
A Bargain Ignoring Uncertainty   48
The Dioxin Case   50
Uncertainty as a Bargaining Resource   55
Bargaining Theory   61
Economic Bargains: Sequential Bargaining with
  Incomplete Information   61
The Principal-Agent Model   62
The Bureaucratic Bargain   64

Chapter 4: Superseding the Bureaucracy   67
The "Outside Option"   70
Strategies for Challenging Scientific Findings   72
Burden of Proof   75
Decisions of the Legislature and Court   77
The Saccharin Case   78
The Dioxin Case   88
Hypothesis   98

Chapter 5: National Comparisons   101
The Government as Regulator and Bargainer   101
National Case Comparisons: Europe and the United States   104
British Opposition to Licensing of Herbicide 2,4,5-T   104
British Opposition to the Siting of the Sizewell B
  Nuclear Power Plant   105
Lack of French Opposition to a Standard for Exposure
  to Vinyl Chloride   106
American Opposition to Licensing of Herbicide 2,4,5-T   108
American Opposition to the Siting of a Nuclear Power
  Plant at Bodega Head, California   108

Contents

American Opposition to a Standard for Exposure to
Vinyl Chloride   110

Comparative Case Findings in Europe and the United
States   111

*Alternative Interpretations: Economic and Political
Institutionalism*   112

*Appendix: National Case Studies in Europe and the United
States*   119

Bibliography   131

Index   147

Preface

This book explains how regulatory decisions change in public health, technological safety, and environmental quality. I examine three primary cases: regulatory decisions on saccharin consumption, dioxin exposure, and liquified natural gas (LNG) exposure (see Appendix of Chapter 1). Six additional cases comparing the United States and Europe are in Chapter 5. My analytic approach is to interpret decision change according to bargains first between regulatory agencies and citizens (or industrialists) and then between those groups and the "outside options"—Congress or the courts. I assume that science is uncertain, and that this is a characteristic of each decision.

I provide an analysis of the types of scientific uncertainty and how they are used to change decisions. Uncertainties occur in extrapolation, data, models, and parameters. Outside options then use these types to create political strategies based on doubtful extrapolation, inadequate data, disputed models, or questionable parameter values. Such strategies change the "burden of proof" (Brooks 1984), by either shifting the *responsibility* of proof (who must prove) or by varying the *standard* of proof (how much must be proved).

Two factors thus drive the analysis of bargaining. The first factor is that citizens or industrialists must organize in opposition to the regulatory decision. If this does not occur, as in the LNG case, then the regulatory decision remains unchanged. The second factor is that the supreme outside option (legislature or highest court) must specifically consider scientific uncertainty. In the dioxin case, the lower court (the first outside option) allowed organized citizens to use scientific uncertainty to successfully oppose the decision. But the upper court (the supreme outside option) reversed this decision of the lower court. It contended that scientific information was sufficient, and that the agency need not demonstrate "scientific unanimity" on the desirability of the decision. By contrast, the regulatory decision on saccharin did change. Citizens protested, and the legislature (the supreme outside option) used scientific uncertainty specifically to erode the decision.

My hypothesis is that when citizens or industrialists organize in protest, and the supreme outside option (legislature or highest court) takes scientific uncertainty into account, then regulatory decisions change. This hypothesis is confirmed by the three additional American case studies in Chapter 5. To explain this hypothesis further it is necessary to compare the United States with Europe. Chapter 5 introduces the French case on vinyl chloride and the British cases on herbicides and nuclear power.

The striking difference between the American and European cases is in the way scientific uncertainty is treated. In the United States, scientific uncertainty is used as a *public* resource and rationale. Scientists work as consultants for public reviews: citizen protests, legislative hearings, and court testimonies. Scientists reveal uncertainties in the science of carcinogenicity and in assessing human health risk. This scientific information is then manipulated by legislators and judges, who change regulatory decisions using these uncertainties in the science.

By contrast, in the European cases, scientific uncertainty is treated as a *private* resource and rationale. French and British scientists never use regulatory decisions as opportunities to reveal scientific uncertainty to the public. Instead, these scientists discuss uncertainties with government officials "behind closed doors." When reports are made to the public about regulatory decisions, scientific information is presented as if it were certain.

The treatment of scientific uncertainty results from a fundamental difference in the nature of the American state versus the European state. This difference is based on the relationship among different branches of the state: the bureaucracy (regulatory agency), legislature, and judiciary (Weber 1958; Brickman et al. 1985). The branches of the American state are *adversarial*, whereas in the French and British states they are *autonomous* from each other. Kitschelt (1989) finds that oversight by the legislature or judicial control by the courts creates conflict in the U.S. state. But Katzenstein (1978) and Krasner (1978) explain that "strong" state institutions in Europe can broker with interest groups without becoming conflictual among branches.

I argue that these differences in the nature of the state explain how scientific uncertainty is ultimately treated. In the United States, bureaucracies try to address or repel involvements by other branches. The outcome is typically supersession within the state. In my three French and British cases, each branch of the state remained autonomous from the others. Neither the parliament (legislature) nor the courts ever opposed a decision by a regulatory agency. Thus, while the U.S. state can supersede its branches using scientific uncertainty, European states instead remain unchanged and consider uncertainty only in private.

I am deeply grateful to Sy D. Friedman, Harvey Brooks, and Harvey Sapolsky for their incisive comments. I also appreciate the help of Peter Cowhey, David Vogel, Richard Lester, and Serge Taylor for their comments on the penultimate draft of this book. Many thanks also to Peter Katzenstein, James Fay, Sheila Jasanoff, Steph Haggard, Larry Susskind, Larry Bacow, John Graham, Gene Rochlin, John Evans, Dorothy Nelkin, Paul Slovic, and Roger Kasperson for their insights on individual chapters. I give thanks to my parents for their profound love, encouragement, and delight in helping hone my thoughts over the years. And I am infinitely grateful to my husband, Sy D. Friedman, without whose commitment, help on logic, and everlasting love and playfulness this book might never have come to fruition. Finally, I would like to thank especially Karen Jones, and also Marsha Orent and Brenda Blais for their beautiful typing of the manuscript.

Bargaining
with
Uncertainty

Chapter One

Bargaining with Uncertainty

What power do citizens have to challenge regulatory decisions? Regulatory agencies are vested with unilateral authority to assure public health, technological safety, and environmental quality. Citizens often feel powerless to voice their specific concerns. Does this regulatory authority over citizens run contrary to our concept of a democratic state? Citizens gain power over regulatory decisions through appeal to Congress and the courts. These superior bodies have statutory rights to assess regulatory behavior through legislative oversight or judicial review.

I describe this interaction according to a bargaining analysis. At the start, subordinate interest groups (citizens, industrialists) try to bargain with governmental bodies (regulatory agencies) that have superior power. To increase their influence, these subordinate groups appeal decisions to a supreme governmental authority: the legislature or court. This "outside option" establishes a second stage of bargaining with higher government authorities. The "payoff" is that regulatory decisions are more likely to change when the legislature or court supersedes the agency.

The key rationale for decision change is scientific uncertainty. Only when scientific evidence is uncertain can citizens and industrialists bargain with the Congress or the courts to constrain regulatory agencies. Scientific uncertainty therefore refers to a significant range of risk estimates by different scientists. Such estimates are based on diverse reasonable assumptions about the data, parameters, and models.

Scientific uncertainty thus also plays an important role in bargaining. Citizens and industrialists use it as a resource to challenge regulatory decisions. Congress and the courts use it to legitimize changes in decisions. Agencies lose their regulatory credibility when decisions must change because scientific information is too uncertain.

In the United States, scientific information is contested by scientists, interest groups, and governmental bodies that bargain vigorously to influence regulatory decisions. By contrast, in Europe national regulatory bureaucracies remain quite autonomous (see Chapter 5). Decisions regarding public health, safety, and the environment are based on a single scientific perspective with no bargaining. Scientists and regulators discuss uncertainties among themselves in private. This difference in public debate of scientific information characterizes the United States as a more open and debating society.

We will develop our analysis by referring to three main cases: (1) the proposed Food and Drug Administration (FDA) ban in 1977 on the consumption of saccharin to prevent risks of cancer (the "saccharin case"); (2) the decision by the New York City Department of Sanitation (DOS) in 1984 to install a municipal waste incinerator in Brooklyn, despite risks of cancer from exposure to dioxin emissions ("the dioxin case"); and (3) the decision of the Federal Power Commission (FPC) (later the Federal Energy Regulatory Commission [FERC]) in 1976 to expand a terminal in Everett, Massachusetts, for transshipment of liquefied natural gas despite risks of fire damage (the "LNG case") (the Appendix following this chapter contains the three case studies in full detail). Another six American and European cases are compared in Chapter 5. Let us first apply the theory to demonstrate what happened in the saccharin case.

BUREAUCRATIC BARGAINING

In developing a model of bargaining, I draw from Terry Moe's (1984, 1987) work on the rational choice theory of relations between legislators and citizens in hierarchical public organizations. Instead of arguing that legislators enact the wishes of citizens, I suggest that both legislators and judges make decisions that change the behavior of bureaucrats and citizens (Weingast 1983; Weingast and Moran 1986a; Bazelon 1981; Abraham and Merrill 1986). I also benefit from the economic game theory of sequential bargaining with incomplete information (Sutton 1986; Fudenberg and Tirole 1983).

My analysis, Bureaucratic Bargaining, specifies the nature and dynamics of bargaining among regulators, scientists, citizens or industrialists, legislators, and judges. It has two stages. In the first stage, the regulatory agency is in the traditional superior role as decisionmaker (Niskanen 1971, 1975). Regulatory statutes give agencies the authority to structure rewards and sanctions for citizens or industrialists to comply with regulations on health, safety, and environmental quality (Moe 1984: 756–757). The agency is obliged to bargain only when citizens and industrialists challenge the information upon which agency decisions are based. Drawing from game theory, the longer the period of offers by bureaucrats and threats (replies) by citizens, the more complete will be the information (Sutton 1986: 717, 719). At a certain point, however, citizens and industrialists stop bargaining and seek a more powerful option.

The second stage of Bureaucratic Bargaining occurs when citizens see the impossibility of a better bargain with the regulatory agency. They exit from bargaining to appeal instead to the superior authority of the legislature or court. This alternative appeal is the "outside option" (Sutton 1986: 712).

I argue that a new bargaining process of rewards and sanctions must now be initiated with legislators or judges in the dominant role (Weingast 1983; Weingast and Moran 1986a: 768–769, 774–775; Bazelon 1981: 212; Abraham and Merrill 1986: 94). Congress retains the right to oversee whether agencies need stricter or weaker standards and procedures. The courts also use judicial reviews (a "hard look") to bolster or curtail information and procedures that agencies use to make decisions (Leventhal 1974; Bazelon 1981: 212).

My hypothesis is that when citizens or industrialists organize in protest, and the supreme outside option (legislature or highest court) takes scientific uncertainty into account, then regulatory bargains change. This hypothesis is confirmed by the additional six cases in Chapter 5.

In light of this analysis of bargaining, let us examine the saccharin case. As the dominant regulatory agency, the FDA began to study the effects of saccharin in 1970 to see whether a preventive decision was needed. The agency was concerned that saccharin might promote the carcinogenicity of other substances in the body (Sapolsky 1986). In 1977 the Canadian Health Protection Branch indicated that 10 percent of test animals fed pure saccharin had contracted bladder tumors (Lecos 1985). By using a straight-line extrapolation to humans, the FDA concluded that normal saccharin use could lead to 1,200 extra bladder cancer cases per year (NRC 1978).

On this basis, the agency proposed a regulatory decision. It recommended in April 1977 that saccharin be banned to prevent use in foods,

beverages, cosmetics, and most drugs. In the report, the FDA referred
to the Delaney Clause of the Food Additives Amendment of 1958, which
requires that the agency identify such carcinogens based on animal tests
or epidemiological data. The National Institutes of Health and the
American Cancer Society supported the FDA's decision.

Such protective regulation should have served most citizens who
preferred not to be exposed to carcinogenic substances. Instead, citizens
and industrialists opposed the regulatory proposal. Vulnerable citizens
spoke out against the ban. These were 10 million diabetics and 60 million
weight watchers who would suffer from lack of a substitute for sugar.
The diet-drink industry joined forces with them. This included major
producers like Royal Crown, Coca-Cola, and Pepsi that primarily
sweetened diet beverages with saccharin.

These groups appealed to Congress to intervene as their outside option.
The American Diabetes Association and the Juvenile Diabetes Association began a national campaign to write letters aimed at members of
Congress. Congress responded immediately to this appeal. Two subcommittees from the Senate and the House of Representatives critically
examined the scientific evidence and arguments considered by the FDA.

Ultimately, Congress imposed a new bargain so that citizens and
industrialists could displace the regulatory agency. Senator Hayakawa of
the Subcommittee on Health and Scientific Research indicated that the
ban on saccharin would be postponed indefinitely, and that the FDA would
be released from responsibility. He recommended, as a substitute, a
market-based labeling requirement, the Saccharin Study and Labeling
Act of November 1977. This act states that saccharin will still be available
for public use, but that warnings of its potential carcinogenic effect are
required on all marketed products. This "Saccharin Moratorium" has
been renewed several times by the Congress, and was still in effect in
1990.

What essential uncertainty in science made this new bargain possible?

SCIENTIFIC UNCERTAINTY AS A RATIONALE

In this book, scientific uncertainty is described by four types: extrapolation, data, model and parameter. These types are important because
legislators and judges use them strategically to delegitimize regulatory
decisions. "Extrapolation" uncertainty occurs when scientists disagree
over whether findings in animal tests can be quantified to assess risks in
humans or not. "Data" uncertainty is when scientists disagree about what
data to use to analyze a risk: numbers of studies, types of samples, or

contradictory findings. "Model" uncertainty occurs when scientists disagree over which parameters should be included in models of risk. Finally, "parameter" uncertainty is when scientists disagree over how to estimate the same parameter within a model.

Science becomes a resource for citizens and industrialists when they use uncertainties in the evidence to question decisions proposed by regulatory agencies. Because evidence remains insufficient to resolve many scientific disputes, citizens and industrialists use their own biases to reinterpret risks as they choose (Jasanoff 1986). Citizens also learn how to use scientific controversies to challenge evidence, undermine analyses, and manipulate knowledge to erode risk estimates of their opponents (Nelkin and Pollack 1979 and1981).

But scientific uncertainty becomes a rationale when supreme governmental bodies delegitimize regulatory decisions. The legislature and court use different political strategies based on the types of scientific uncertainty. Disputes arise among regulators, scientific consultants, and members of Congress or judges as they try to interpret uncertain scientific evidence.

In the saccharin case, scientists faced three types of scientific uncertainty: extrapolation, data, and model. Extrapolation from rat tests led to estimates of cancer risk varying over three orders of magnitude (NRC 1978: 3–71, 3–72). Epidemiological data gave the National Academy of Sciences (NAS) little reason to believe that saccharin would cause cancer directly. The choice of model was also controversial. Was saccharin to be modeled as a promoter or as an initiator of cancer? The key question was whether it interacted synergistically with smoking, or instead initiated bladder cancer on its own. Another model uncertainty was whether the latency period of 20 to 40 years would hide the rise in rates of cancer in the population assessed over shorter time periods. As a result of these scientific uncertainties, the NAS was not prepared to draw conclusions about whether saccharin was a carcinogenic risk to humans, although it was more lenient on animal effects.

Citizens and industrialists attempted to use such uncertainties as resources in bargaining. They tried to discredit FDA procedures using attacks on data such as sample size. Citizens joined with the Calorie Control Council (CCC), representing the diet-drink industry, to challenge the agency's findings. The CCC had hired scientific consultants who pointed out that massive overdoses of saccharin to animals in the Canadian study were not equivalent to the high doses of saccharin that a person would consume. Despite the FDA's retort that high doses overcompensated for an insufficiently large sample size, the CCC was determined to shake the regulatory agency's basis of scientific judgment. Ultimately, however, both citizens and industrialists had to appeal to Congress to change the decision. The congressional Office of Technology Assessment (OTA) issued a report in 1977 about the saccharin controversy. Although the report concluded that saccharin was a potential human carcinogen, it stated firmly that "there are no reliable quantitative estimates of the risk" (Office of Technology Assessment 1977).

Two subcommittee hearings in the Senate and the House of Representatives then developed the bargaining rationales for delaying the FDA decision. These rationales emphasized extrapolation, data, and model uncertainty. Concerning extrapolation from rat tests to human risk, members of congress asked scientists from the FDA whether the methodology of extrapolation was well enough developed to assess quantitative risks in humans. Could one extrapolate from a "weak" animal carcinogen to assess a level of human risk? Uncertainties about data were also questioned. The representative in the hearing by the House Subcommittee claimed that the FDA's Canadian study of epidemiology was deficient because the data sample was too small. Meanwhile, the senator in the Senate subcommittee hearing shifted the discussion of saccharin to a discussion of the impurities associated with saccharin. The senator created a hypothetical argument about how impurities could be found to be carcinogens. This argument helped to protect saccharin from further investigation. Congress also discussed the issue of latency, thereby raising uncertainty about the choice of model. Such political disputes over extrapolation, data, and models were used by representatives and senators who wanted to fully exploit scientific uncertainties to challenge the basis of the FDA's decision. These disputes ultimately convinced Congress that a ban was not needed.

The emergent bargain effectively changed the regulatory decision by postponing it indefinitely. Citizen groups, NAS scientists, and industrialists used the outside option of Congress to oppose how the FDA employed uncertain science. How does this bargain compare to those in the LNG and dioxin cases?

ALTERNATIVE CASE STUDIES

In the LNG case, the Federal Power Commission prepared a Final Environmental Impact Statement (FEIS) in 1976 to justify expanding the LNG terminal in Everett, Massachusetts. They hired a research firm to do a conditional probability accident model. This model showed how negligible were the health risks from a possible fire if the LNG were to explode. Although scientists from MIT and Harvard questioned the scientific information, no outside option intervened to change the decision. Scientists doubted the modeling of dense gas movement (LNG) and uses of statistical methods. Although a small group protested, most Everett residents were ready to comply with the agency's control of decision-making. These residents did not call in the legislature or court to represent the uncertainties noted by scientists. Instead, the residents gave the FPC overwhelming support in 1976 for the bargain: expansion of the LNG terminal. Their hopes were that jobs and services might grow as a result.

By contrast, in the dioxin case, Brooklyn, New York, residents were ready to sue in court to stop construction of a municipal waste incinerator facility. In 1984 the Department of Sanitation of New York City responded to the trash crisis by preparing a Draft Environmental Impact Statement to build a mass-burn facility to incinerate the city's solid waste. Fred Hart Co. produced a report that estimated only 6 additional cancer deaths per million people exposed to facility emissions of dioxin over a 70-year lifetime.

Scientist Barry Commoner and the Hasidic community of Williamsburg joined forces. Commoner estimated that the actual number of additional cancer deaths could be over two orders of magnitude greater than Hart's estimate. The Hasidic community (adjacent to the site) and two other Brooklyn Community Districts protested the site choice. These residents finally filed a lawsuit against the DOS in the Supreme Court of New York City to stop construction of the facility, and they won. They won because their lawyer used Commoner's scientific evidence to challenge the court. But the residents lost when the case was appealed to the higher Appellate Division in July 1985. In that supreme outside option, no scientific uncertainty was given legitimacy. The court approved the earlier decision, and simply neglected the need for "scientific unanimity."

These two cases reveal diametrically opposed approaches to bargaining. Residents in the LNG case were unwilling to demand that Congress or the courts intervene using the scientific uncertainties of the Harvard and MIT scientists. Instead, residents favored the terminal as desired by the regulatory agency. By contrast, the courts did intervene in the dioxin case, but the supreme Appellate Court did not allow scientific uncertainty to be considered. Williamsburg residents and other local residents used the scientific uncertainty provided by Commoner only to sue the DOS in the lower court. But the supreme outside option did not allow those residents to use scientific uncertainty to reverse the regulatory decision.

The bargains that resulted, therefore, were either postponed indefinitely (saccharin), reversed (dioxin), or never changed (LNG). How do we explain this?

OUTLINE OF THE BOOK

This chapter has introduced the context of regulatory decision-making in public health, technological safety, and environmental quality in the United States. The legislature and courts bargain using scientific uncertainty to supersede decisions made by regulatory agencies. The Appendix to this chapter reviews the three primary case studies.

Chapter 2 analyzes four types of scientific uncertainty in depth. In the LNG case, a leading expert at MIT used model uncertainty to challenge the exclusion of a key parameter from the Federal Power Commission's model of dense gas dispersion. In the dioxin case, a biologist used parameter uncertainty to criticize the Department of Sanitation's measure of a central variable in the model. As we have discussed in the saccharin case, reputable scientists challenged the Food and Drug Administration's use of extrapolation, its neglect of data, and choice of model.

Chapter 3 develops the bargaining analysis, the "Bureaucratic Bargain." It explains in detail how citizens and industrialists used scientific uncertainty to try to extract concessions from regulatory agencies on decisions. Despite a strong effort by the opposing scientist, local Everett residents in the LNG case were *not* concerned about the rare chance of a dangerous LNG explosion. Residents never pressured the agency to change its traditional bargain of citizen compliance. By contrast, a confrontation did occur in the dioxin case. Local residents joined an opposing scientist to try to prevent construction of the incinerator. In the first stage of bargaining, no compromise agreement was ever achieved. Citizens were unwilling to tolerate any risk of inducing cancer over a lifetime.

Chapter 4 looks at the key second stage of bargaining. This is when the legislature or the court decides that it must supersede the authority of the regulatory agency to reach a regulatory bargain. The oversight of Congress enabled it to use scientific uncertainty to supersede the regulatory decision of the agency in the saccharin case. In the dioxin case, the lower Supreme Court of New York threatened the regulatory agency with having performed an Environmental Impact Review that was scientifically inadequate. But the higher Appellate Division reversed this threat, stating that the scientific information at hand need not be examined to any greater extent. These two cases suggest that the ability of supervisory bodies to supersede agencies depends upon how powerfully scientific uncertainty is used to change or retain a bargained decision.

Chapter 5 compares regulatory decisions in Europe with those in the United States. Six new cases discuss the regulation of herbicides and the siting of nuclear power plants in Britain and the United States, and the regulation of vinyl chloride in France and the United States. These cases are presented in detail in the Appendix to that chapter. I find that in Europe, regulatory agencies remain in charge and scientists seldom get involved in public bargaining. This is a stark contrast to the United States, where legislatures and courts often supersede regulatory agencies. Chapter 5 recapitulates the entire theory as demonstrated by the nine case studies in the United States and Europe. I also discuss what the comparative evidence suggests for the nature of the democratic state.

APPENDIX: THE PRIMARY CASE STUDIES

The case studies in this book cover a wide range of decisions to regulate public health, technological safety, and environmental quality. Three primary cases provide the evidence upon which the bureaucratic argument is based. These cases examine responses of officials and interest groups to agency proposals for decisions that would (1) increase fire risks by expanding a liquefied natural gas terminal in Everett, Massachusetts; (2) increase risks of cancer from exposure to dioxin emissions by building a municipal waste incinerator in Brooklyn, New York; and (3) prevent cancer risks by banning the consumption of saccharin in the United States.

These risks are quite different in their characteristics. Some risks like consuming saccharin in diet drinks are taken willingly. Others like being exposed to dioxin emissions are involuntary. Some risks like a widespread LNG fire are potential catastrophes. Others like consuming saccharin are small effects accumulated over a long period of time. Some like exposure to an LNG accident are imminent, while others like dioxin exposure from a proposed incinerator are future risks only to be experienced toward the end of a lifetime. Drinking a saccharin-sweetened beverage is a risk that is taken individually. Another risk like suffering burns during an LNG fire may affect a great number of people at once. While some risks such as saccharin consumption can be personally monitored and controlled, others like a leak releasing LNG onto harbor waters are extremely difficult to predict and prevent. Cancer from exposure to dioxin compounds is a relatively "new" risk for some people. The risk of injury from an LNG fire is more familiar to others.

Other natural, cultural, political, and economic factors may also be important in determining whether groups oppose agencies or not. For example, do residents oppose an agency that converts natural gas into an ignitable liquid in order to transport it easier? Did a religious organization against dioxin risks determine the extent of protest in that case? Was the well-organized lobbying of the American Diabetes Association against a saccharin ban independent of any concern about uncertainties in the scientific research on its carcinogenic effects? Such diverse factors partly obscure our effort to understand the extent that disagreements among experts incite groups to oppose agency decisions.

Despite these idiosyncratic features, some characteristics common to the cases justify their comparison here. First, citizens' reactions to agency proposals were strongly influenced by political or ideological motivations. Second, the legislature or courts used citizen appeals to jeopardize regulatory decisions proposed. Third, scientific uncertainty was the key factor used to jeopardize decisions. Let us turn to the case evidence.

Relative Uncertainty about the Fire Risks of Licensing a Liquefied Natural Gas Import Terminal in Boston Harbor (the LNG Case)

Liquefied natural gas is natural gas that has been cooled to -259° F, reducing its volume over 600 times to facilitate transport by tanker. A leak in a transport tank can release the liquid into the air or onto water or soil. Any ignition source can then cause an instantaneous fire (or explosion) during the time it takes the liquid to heat and expand to a natural gas vapor 630 cubic feet larger.

During the period 1971 to 1985, Distrigas, a Massachusetts subsidiary of the privately owned Cabot Corporation, operated a liquefied natural gas import terminal on the shores of the Boston Harbor, near the town of Everett. At the start, the Federal Power Commission (later the Federal Energy Regulatory Commission) claimed that the onshore operations at Everett did not fall within its jurisdiction of interstate commerce. But when Distrigas applied to extend its distribution outside Massachusetts, the FPC did claim jurisdiction. The agency required in 1973 that Distrigas obtain permits for the construction and operation of the terminal, the import of LNG from Algeria, and its sale in interstate commerce.

The FPC prepared a Draft Environmental Impact Statement (DIES) for the terminal in 1973. The agency staff commissioned Science Applications, Inc. (SAI) to perform a risk assessment of the probability of a marine accident involving collision, ramming, or grounding in Boston Harbor, the waterway to Everett. Onshore transshipment, trucking, barging, and pipeline accidents were excluded, since they fell under the jurisdiction of the Department of Transportation and the U.S. Coast Guard. The FPC staff was therefore concerned only whether a tanker accident, LNG spill, formation of an LNG vapor cloud, and ignition of the cloud would cause fatalities from direct exposure to the ensuing fire and radiation.

SAI used a conditional probability accident model to assess these overall health risks. The risk of fatalities per exposed person per year was assessed by multiplying the probabilities of (1) a tanker casualty, (2) an LNG spill in the event of a tanker accident, (3) the formation of a vapor cloud and subsequent ignition of the cloud, and (4) human casualties from exposure to the vapor cloud.

Based primarily on this risk assessment, the Final Environmental Impact Statement filed by the FPC in 1976 estimated that health and safety risks were negligible. The estimate of the worst case was that one tank of LNG would leak and the resulting LNG pool would immediately ignite. This would result in an individual risk (fatalities per exposed person per year) of only about 2 in 10 million (2.63×10^{-7}). The frequency of this event was expected once every 77,500 years (FPC 1976: 3–11). Given a worst-case spill caused by a tanker grounding, the maximum number of fatalities was estimated to be 2,500 to 3,500 people. Lacking its own guideline or standard, the FPC considered these risks to be acceptable according to the criterion of less than one in a hundred thousand (10^{-5}) developed by the Electric Power Research Institute (EPRI) from studies of voluntary and involuntary exposure to risk (FPC 1976).

Scientific uncertainty about FPC estimates, however, was revealed by Professors James Fay, a specialist on dense gases in MIT's Department of Mechanical Engineering, and William Fairley of Harvard's Department of Statistics. In their review of the DEIS, these experts claimed that the estimates were based on questionable modeling of dense gas (LNG) movement and inappropriate uses of statistical methods. Data were insufficient to estimate the occurrence of an LNG fire using statistical means. As a result, the risk of fatalities might be underestimated by almost an order of magnitude (a factor of ten) bringing the estimate closer to the threshold of unacceptable risk according to EPRI (Fay 1976). The scientific evidence and theory presented by these experts fueled local protest.

The Massachusetts branch of the protest group BLAST (Bring Legal Action to Stop the Tanks), was formed in the early 1970s. It originated as a response to the national ("60 Minutes") and local media coverage of the operations in Everett. Certainly the issues raised particularly by Fay served to fuel the concerns of MassBLAST. But the group always remained quite small, so that its effect in opposing the FPC was minimal. Instead, the general willingness of Everett citizens to comply first with the aldermen in Everett in 1969 and then with the FPC in 1976 gave overwhelming support to the proposed expansion of the terminal.

Residents thus posed little opposition to the FPC's proposal to increase safety risks by expanding the terminal. This was in stark contrast to the case of dioxin. There, residents strongly opposed agency proposals to increase cancer risks by siting a municipal waste incinerator in their neighborhood. The risks of cancer estimated by scientists, however, ranged between low and high levels.

High Uncertainty about Estimates of Dioxin Risks Posed by Municipal Waste Incineration in New York City (the Dioxin Case)

Dioxin emissions are different from LNG in that they are a continuous but low exposure to a health hazard. But they are similar to LNG in that dioxin risks are involuntary, owing to a man-made source, are relatively "new," and are perceived to be "catastrophic." Perhaps most important, dioxin risks were only *proposed* in this case, and might therefore have been eliminated by a strong opposition. In the LNG case, the risk already existed, making it more difficult to eliminate entirely.

Dioxins are polychlorinated isomers that form as by-products either during combustion of waste products or afterward in the incinerator stack. They include dibenzo-dioxins (PCDD), dibenzofurans (PCDF), and 2,3,7,8-tetrachlorodibeno-p-dioxin (TCDD). 2,3,7,8-TCDD is one of the extremely carcinogenic groups of dioxin compounds. A risk of exposure to humans occurs once dioxin compounds are released from the stack of the incinerator and are transported by the wind elsewhere. The dose of dioxin to which an individual is exposed depends on the daily intake of dioxin based on concentrations in the air inhaled or the water, soil, or dust consumed by the individual.

New York City's population of 12 million generates about 26,000 tons of garbage per day. Of the six sites in New York and New Jersey used to landfill this refuse, five reached full capacity by 1989. All are currently leaking pollutants into the surrounding groundwater. The U.S. Environmental Protection Agency (EPA) has warned that these sites must be renovated or shut down to comply with the Clean Water Act of 1970.

The New York Department of Sanitation responded to this crisis by recommending in 1984 that seven to ten Resource Recovery Facilities (RRF) be built over the next five to ten years to incinerate the city's solid waste. The first facility would use a mass-burn technology to reduce the volume and weight of a maximum of 3,000 tons per day of municipal solid waste. The Brooklyn Navy Yard site was selected because of its environmental characteristics, ownership of the land by the city, and direct access to the citywide waste barging system.

DOS prepared a Draft Environmental Impact Statement in 1984. Public concern over dioxin emissions from the proposed Brooklyn Navy Yard facility led the agency to commission a study of the potential health risks. In 1984, Fred C. Hart Associates, Inc., produced the health risk study, the "Assessment of Potential Public Health Impacts Associated with Predicted Emissions of Polychlorinated Dibenzo-Furans (PCDF) from the Brooklyn Navy Yard Resource Recovery Facility." This document, the "Hart Report," included a risk assessment that computed a worst case upper bound on the probability of human cancer associated with maximum rates of dioxin emissions. The report estimated that the worst case was an insignificant level of only six additional cancer deaths per million people exposed to facility emissions over a 70-year lifetime (Hart 1984). These cases were in addition to those expected due to the existing cancer mortality rate of about 21 percent in the population.

But the scientific uncertainty underlying this risk estimate did not go unchallenged. Barry Commoner and his associates instead estimated a much higher worst case of 1,430 additional cancer cases per million people exposed to the facility over a lifetime. This estimate was two orders of magnitude higher than the six additional cancer cases predicted in the Hart Report. Commoner's assumptions differed from Hart's in that he assumed that dioxin compounds *could* be formed in the stack at lower temperatures, rather than only in the combustion chamber (where they would be destroyed by the higher temperatures). These assumptions justified the use of data showing much higher rates of dioxin emissions from incinerators (Commoner et al. 1984).

Commoner investigated the problem at the request of the Hasidic community in Williamsburg (adjacent to the site) and two other Brooklyn Community Districts. Together they formed an organization called "Coalition for a Safe Environment." The Coalition was concerned that the health risks of residents might be higher than reported by the DOS. When confronted with the significant discrepancy between the Commoner and Hart cancer estimates, the residents physically protested the siting of the incinerator.

Faced with this controversy, the Board of Estimate (BOE) called in the New York Academy of Sciences to mediate. A group from MIT led a one-day session involving representatives from the DOS, the Brooklyn Community Districts, members of the scientific community, and other concerned groups. The session concluded with an understanding that the siting of the incinerator would give Community Districts guarantees of compensation, insurance, and monitoring of the facility.

But only months later this understanding had dissolved. In August 1985 the BOE approved the facility with a 6–5 vote, despite a 100 percent vote against the facility by the advisory groups of the three Community Boards of Brooklyn (including Williamsburg). Residents filed a lawsuit against the DOS in the Supreme Court of New York in order to stop construction of the facility, and won. But these same residents lost when the case was appealed in the higher Appellate Division in July 1985. By September 1986, adjudicatory hearings by the New York Department of Conservation regarding construction and operating permits were delayed owing to a conflict-of-interest charge against the trial judge. Although the charge was initially upheld in the New York Supreme Court, it was later reversed by the Appellate Division (Meyer interview 6/24/87).

In the dioxin case, groups were very strongly opposed to the DOS proposal to increase cancer risks. This opposition was similar to that of consumers in the saccharin case. In the saccharin case, however, consumers opposed the agency's effort to reduce cancer risks, while in the dioxin case, residents insisted upon it.

High Uncertainty about Estimates of Cancer Risks for Consumption of Saccharin (the Saccharin Case)

The saccharin case is different from the other cases in that it is a product whose consumption in diet foods and beverages is voluntary, individual, and not new. Despite these differences, however, our discussion has already shown that disputes among experts were important in fomenting opposition to the ban. The following analysis provides more empirical detail about the case.

Saccharin is a nonnutritive sweetener that provides no calories. It is chemically derived from coal tar. Unlike most other carcinogens, saccharin neither changes chemically in the body nor attaches to genes, and it is excreted rapidly. It tends to promote the carcinogenic effect of other substances in the body rather than to initiate cancer directly (Sapolsky 1986).

Over 70 million Americans are exposed to saccharin by consuming it directly as an artificial sweetener or indirectly as a sweetener in foods, beverages, cosmetics, and most drugs (Sapolsky 1986). Until 1969 when cyclamate was banned, the two had been generally used in a combination of ten parts cyclamate to one part saccharin. But since then, Royal Crown's Diet Rite Cola, Coca-Cola's Tab, and Diet Pepsi have all been sweetened primarily with saccharin. The largest group at risk from saccharin are about 60 million weight watchers.

The FDA began to study the cancer risks of saccharin in 1970 upon the recommendation of the National Research Council of the National Academy of Sciences. Since 1958, saccharin, similar to cyclamate, had been listed on the FDA's list of food additives "generally recognized as safe" (the GRAS list) with virtually no testing. Evidence in studies of cyclamate, however, suggested that saccharin might also be a carcinogen. As a result of this evidence, in April 1977 the FDA therefore recommended that saccharin be banned from use in foods, beverages, cosmetics, and most drugs. But the National Academy of Sciences was not prepared to draw conclusions about whether saccharin was carcinogenic. Epidemiological studies showed no link between the consumption of saccharin and bladder cancer.

The Calorie Control Council, representative of the soft-drink companies, also challenged the FDA's findings. Its experts pointed out that the massive overdoses of saccharin in the Canadian study were not equivalent to any quantity possibly consumed by a person. The American Diabetes Association and the Juvenile Diabetes Association, spurred on by the diet-drink industry, began a national letter-writing campaign aimed at the FDA and members of Congress.

Based on the Office of Technology Assessment report and public outcry, two subcommittees from the Senate and the House of Representatives examined the scientific evidence and arguments. Expressing concern for those on restricted sugar diets, members of Congress called for a postponement of the ban, and recommended the Saccharin Study and Labeling Act, which was signed in November 1977 (U.S. Congress 1977). The act states that saccharin will still be available for public use, but that warnings of its carcinogenic effect are required on all marketed products. The Saccharin Moratorium has been renewed several times and was still in effect as of 1990.

Chapter Two

Uncertain Science

One would expect that controversies among scientists over the evidence of health risk would cause bureaucrats to revise prior decisions. Quite the contrary: the last two decades show that many agency decisions remain unchanged despite vociferous disagreements among scientists over the facts.

Much of the body of accumulated scientific knowledge in the physical sciences is relatively certain. No one is trying to revise the table of basic chemical elements or to discover a new formula for gravitational attraction. However, in the health sciences, the span of certain knowledge is much more limited. Scientists still disagree about whether all doses or only cumulative "threshold" doses of chemicals like ethylene thiourea over time initiate cancer (Ricci and Molton 1985: 475). M. Granger Morgan et al. (1984: 201–215) show in a study of sulfur air pollution how diverse were the models of health damage due to exposure. The variation of estimates of adverse effects ranged from zero to a few thousand excess deaths per year. Uncertainties in data, models, and theories prevail as scientists and bureaucrats decide how to protect the public.

This chapter has three purposes. The first is to clarify what Congress intended regulatory agencies to do to protect the public from harm. I compare the legislative mandates of agencies. The second purpose is to describe what regulatory agencies and their scientific consultants actually did. The section reviews how risk was assessed by agency scientists in three cases: decisions on saccharin, dioxin, and liquefied natural gas.

The final purpose of the chapter is to discuss the challenges posed by scientists not assisting the agency. The section emphasizes the adversarial institutional settings, alternative roles of scientists, different critiques of risk, and the types of scientific uncertainties upon which opposing scientists relied. The three case studies show how consistently controversy arose over scientific issues.

STATUTORY REQUIREMENTS TO EXAMINE SCIENCE

Perhaps the most important legislation on the role of scientific information is the 1946 Administrative Procedures Act. According to this act, an agency must state the source of its scientific information and the relationship between that information and the decision it proposes. The agency is instructed to provide the public with the methods whereby citizens can gain scientific information about decisions. Citizens are also to be provided full statements of the scope of all reports or examinations, the agency's general policy, and its adopted procedures for interpreting evidence (U.S. Congress 1946: 68–147). Full information disclosure is the procedural rule and secrecy the exception (Wellford v. Hardin 1970) Even if information is incomprehensible to ordinary citizens, agencies must still disclose the entire extent of the information (Robles v. Environmental Protection Agency 1973). Of special interest here is that all purely factual information is required to be released to the public (U.S. v. J.B. Williams Co., Inc. 1975).

One point is raised here because it becomes particularly important in Chapter 4. The purpose of the Administrative Procedures Act (APA) is to instruct the regulatory agency how to use scientific information to set protective standards. The purpose of setting such a "burden of proof" is to indicate which party—polluter or citizen—is responsible to provide a proof of harm or safety, and with what standard of proof. Statutes of the National Environmental Policy Act (NEPA) and the State Environmental Quality Review Act (SEQRA) did not identify who had the burden of proof (NEPA 1969; SEQRA 1976). The statute on food additives, however, instructed that the manufacturer was responsible.

A key issue is how to treat scientific uncertainty. This appears to vary across national and state legislatures. The first compares statutes on environmental policy in both federal and state jurisdictions. The second compares different policies—here, environment and food additives—in the same federal jurisdiction.

Environmental Policy: Federal versus State Mandates

In the LNG case, the Federal Power Commission filed a Final Environmental Impact Statement in 1976 consistent with the demand of the U.S. Congress that federal agencies protect the environment according to NEPA of 1969. In the dioxin case, New York City's Department of Sanitation filed a FEIS in 1985 in order to comply with the legislative demand that state agencies protect the environment according to SEQRA of 1976. Although the DOS also had to satisfy the requirements of New York City's environmental policy act, it is not discussed here.

The comprehensive purposes of both federal and state acts were similar. Both were aimed to prevent or eliminate damage to the environment, and either to stimulate the health and welfare of man (NEPA 1969: 523) or to enrich ecological, natural, human, and community resources (SEQRA 1976: 60). Both laws also stated that all agencies should develop detailed statements identifying environmental impacts, adverse environmental effects, alternatives, relationships between short-term uses and long-term productivity, and irreversible commitments of resources (NEPA 1969: 553–554; SEQRA 1976: 69).

NEPA (p. 529) instructs that regulators should "declare a national policy . . . [promote] harmony between man and his environment . . . prevent or eliminate damage to the environment . . . and stimulate the health and welfare of man." SEQRA (p. 62) also instructs that "maintaining . . . of a quality environment . . . is healthful and pleasing to the senses . . . now and in the future."

Judges clarified, however, that NEPA should be dismissed from dealing with issues like scientific uncertainty, while SEQRA would still be responsible. At the national level, Environmental Impact Statements (EISs) were not expected to do what was "scientifically impossible" (Natural Resources Defense Council, Inc. v. Callaway 1974). Nor was the "sum total of scientific knowledge" required in EISs (Columbia Basin Land Protection Association v. Kleppe 1976). Moreover, technical information that was "too uncertain" could simply be eliminated from EISs (City of Romulus v. Wayne County 1975).

Judges determined that "scientific perfection" and "scientific unanimity" were not necessary. Experts could disagree with each other's risk estimates, and agencies could still make satisfactory decisions (Movement Against Destruction v. Trainor 1975). The number of court tests of scientific disputes according to NEPA has been large. Nevertheless, the ability of the agency is to decide upon which scientific evidence to base its decision, and upon which to dismiss from review owing to uncertainty.

By contrast, proponents of projects at the state level were still told to consider *all* of the available scientific information. Agencies had to "consider fully" all of the environmental consequences revealed in EISs and to make decisions on actions based on this information (Town of Henrietta v. Department of Environmental Conservation of New York 1980). This strictness of SEQRA may have been partly a result of the smaller number of legal tests by courts, compared to the situation of NEPA. In fact, regarding scientific unanimity, the court was more lenient on contestants. Scientists could disagree with the action proposed by an agency, and yet the agency decision would still be satisfactory (Matter of Environmental Defense Fund v. Flacke 1983). This suggests that SEQRA is obliged to fully consider the evidence, but that disputes indicating scientific uncertainty could dismiss that evidence.

This difference between the legal treatment of scientific uncertainty was stark in the national NEPA and state SEQRA cases. At the national level, the agency was free to dismiss scientific uncertainty. It could choose upon which scientific evidence to base its decision. But at the state level, the agency was directed to consider the scientific uncertainty. SEQRA indicated that the agency must fully consider the evidence of uncertainty.

Food Additives versus Environmental Policies: Federal Mandates

In the saccharin case, the FDA filed a proposal to ban saccharin because the chemical had proven carcinogenic in test animals and, based on extrapolations, was probably carcinogenic in humans. This was consistent with Section 348 of the Food Additives Amendment of 1958, known as the "Delaney Clause," which indicates that "no additive shall be deemed to be safe if it is found to induce cancer when ingested by man or animal." [Food Additives Amendment of 1958, Sect. 348 (c) (A)]. As head of the Select Committee on Food Additives, Representative James Delaney, a Democrat from New York State, had managed to push this clause through the House of Representatives in 1958 so that it became part of the amendment. The Delaney Clause thus stated very specifically that any evidence of carcinogenic effects even in rats was unacceptable. By contrast, NEPA remained entrenched in its broad, unspecified review of overall environmental and health effects.

Congress appears to have been consistent across the two cases regarding the treatment of scientific uncertainty. In NEPA, the legislature indicated that the agency was *free* to dismiss the uncertainty. It was able to choose upon which scientific evidence to base its decision. In Delaney, the agency was *told* to dismiss the scientific uncertainty. It was directed to base its decision on minimal evidence of carcinogenicity—one positive test on rats was sufficient. All of the remaining scientific evidence was to be eliminated from consideration.

In court, decisions were made that reinforced the Delaney Clause and its strict interpretation, even if scientists were highly certain about their own findings of carcinogenicity in rats. One court, for example, stated that the FDA had to apply the Delaney Clause even if the carcinogenic effect was only produced in one strain of test animal rather than in all experiments (Bell v. Goddard 1966). Another court decided that agencies should be strict about granting permission for the use of chemicals even if they only apparently produced cancer in animals (Environmental Defense Fund, Inc. v. Ruckelshaus 1971). Such strict enforcement of the Delaney Clause by the courts reinforced the conviction of the FDA that statutory decisions were legally required.

Whereas NEPA allowed scientific uncertainty to be dismissed, the Delaney Clause focused insistently on one positive carcinogenic test on rats. SEQRA remained in between these two legislations. What effect have these quite different interpretations had on the actual risk assessments performed by agency scientists?

RISK ASSESSMENT BY AGENCY SCIENTISTS

According to their statutes, the FDA, the DOS, and the FPC were asked to make valid scientific judgments of sparse evidence. The FDA made a conservative decision based on evidence of carcinogenicity in rats. The DOS made a radical decision by using a risk assessment based on an insufficient body of data. The third agency, the FPC, was not even required by statute to make a scientific decision. Still, like the DOS, that agency chose to use a risk assessment methodology despite sparse evidence. The following three case studies explain these discontinuities between statutory requirements and risk assessments based on fragmentary scientific evidence.

The Saccharin Case

The strict Delaney Clause forced the FDA to judge human cancer risk based on any positive findings in animal tests. The agency was therefore compelled in 1977 to analyze animal tests. Insufficient research had been done, and saccharin was still not clearly dissociated from other potential causes of carcinogenic effects such as impurities.

The agency had done its own animal studies: U.S. Department of Health, Education and Welfare (USDHEW 1973), the Wisconsin Alumni Research Foundation (WARF 1973), and a more recent output of the the Canadian government's National Health and Welfare Ministry (CNHWM 1977). These suggested that saccharin might be a weak human carcinogen. To extrapolate from animal tests to human incidence required a couple of scientific steps. First, evidence in the experimental tests had to show that animals fed extremely high doses of saccharin did initiate cancer. And second, that extrapolating from such immediate, high-dose animal studies did suggest that saccharin could be a carcinogen, given long-term, low doses in humans.

To take the first step, the studies mentioned above did two-generation analyses of saccharin consumption (and impurities) by rats (NRC 1978: 3–18, 3–19). The two-generation structure enabled scientists also to study the effect of metabolites both from mothers' milk and also from the diet. In each study, rats of each sex of the parent generation were fed saccharin in their diets from weaning through pregnancy and preweaning of their offspring. The offspring generation was placed on the same diet as their parents for their entire lifespan. The following dose levels of saccharin were used in the studies: gradations of 0.01 through 7.5 percent in the FDA study, 0.05 through 5 percent in the WARF study, and 5 percent in the Canadian study (USDHEW 1973; WARF 1973; CNHWM 1977).

The incidence of bladder tumors in males of the offspring generation treated with saccharin at the highest dose levels was consistently higher than that of control groups. In the WARF study, 8 out of 14 treated males developed bladder cancer. The FDA (USDHEW) study showed seven cases of bladder cancer out of the total of 23 males given doses of saccharin. The Canadian study demonstrated that 7 out of 38 males initiated bladder cancer. In all three studies, control groups of nearly the same size exhibited zero or one case of cancer in males (WARF 1973; USDHEW 1973; CNHWM 1977; NRC 1978, Table 3-2). These findings led the FDA to assert with some confidence that saccharin was a carcinogen in male offspring.

The second step for the FDA focused on whether saccharin was a carcinogen in humans. Animal studies properly conducted are assumed by many scientists to qualitatively predict human responses to carcinogens. Where the difference in judgment lies, however, is in whether such studies can also be used to quantify human risk levels. Extrapolation consists of two basic calculations: extrapolating from high-dose to low-dose levels in test animals, and extrapolating estimated risks for animals at low doses to risks for humans at comparable levels.

One of the most controversial aspects is the choice of the dose-response model, which correlates a dose level with an observable response in the animal. The problem is that there are many competing models, and they vary distinctively at low-dose levels. The most commonly used models differ by about a 200-fold dose range. This is quite a substantial scientific uncertainty in interpreting sparse evidence of low-dose effects.

Besides extrapolation, the method of adjusting doses between species is also quite uncertain. Extrapolating between rats and humans is based on debatable "equivalent-dose" rules. Various methods include expressing dose as a percent of the daily diet, a proportion of body weight, or as a rapport between total lifetime ingestion and the unit of body weight (NRC 1978: 3-61/3-75). Scientists have little consensus about which method is the most valid.

The FDA ran into a considerable range of possible values when it estimated the human risk extrapolated from its animal tests (WARF 1973; USDHEW 1973; CNHWM 1977). Allowing both equivalent-dose and dose-response models to vary, the FDA estimated the number of human cancer cases per million people exposed to saccharin (at 0.12 grams/day) over a lifetime to be between 0.001 to 5,200 cases! There was no clear bunching of the variation toward one or the other estimate (NRC 1978: 3-71, 3-72).

Faced with such uncertainty in the calculations, the FDA was careful to make its risk estimate of human exposure to saccharin. Exercising conservatism, the FDA scientists judged that a straight-line extrapolation from animal tests indicated that anywhere from zero to 1,200 incremental additional cases of bladder cancer per year might be the best estimate of cancer risk from human consumption of saccharin. The statistical uncertainty in these extrapolations was likely to cause any precise value to be incorrect by a factor of ten (one order of magnitude) (Kennedy testimony in Subcommittee on Health and Scientific Research 1977:101).

The FDA assumed, however, that about 50-70 million Americans consume products containing saccharin. This would mean that although the dose was low, the number of people affected within the U.S. population was large. The agency therefore assessed the magnitude of exposure of the population to be high despite the weak effect on a per capita basis (McCann scientific testimony, Subcommittee on Health and Scientific Research 1977:66).

Thus, the FDA's estimate of risk from consuming saccharin was far from certain. The estimate ranged over three orders of magnitude, with a single order attributed to the statistical uncertainty in the estimation process and in the scientific evidence. Given insufficient data, how could scientists hired by the DOS in the dioxin case be any more certain of their risk estimates regarding dioxin exposure?

The Dioxin Case

The New York City Department of Sanitation was also burdened by a state environmental law, which demanded that uncertain science be taken into account. Moreover, the agency was faced with a morass of sparse and poorly understood data on the health effects of dioxin. Both the DOS and its scientific consulting firm, the John Hart Company, were hard-pressed to generate reliable estimates of cancer risk. But instead of being satisfied as was the FDA with imprecise estimates, the DOS used its EIS to report precise calculations of the risk of human cancer from dioxin exposure.

In its Draft Environmental Impact Statement, the DOS started off by covering standard requirements for evaluating the impacts of a proposed siting project. The report analyzed land use, air quality, noise, water, transportation, utilities, economic impact, alternatives, and mitigation measures. But following criticism from a nonagency scientist, Dr. Barry Commoner, the DOS was compelled to hire other scientists at the John Hart Company to bolster the agency's technical assessment of exposure to dioxin emissions. These dioxin compounds included polychlorinated dibenzo-dioxins (PCDD), polychlorinated dibenzo-furans (PCDF), and 2,3,7,8-tetrachlorodibenzo-dioxin (2,3,7,8-TCDD).

The DOS appears ultimately to have implemented a two-pronged strategy to deal with the controversial issue of dioxin threats to health. The DEIS treated dioxin problems in a minimal review. The Hart report then proceeded to deal with exposure as a highly technical problem. It used a methodology of precise estimation of risk and assessment of health impacts even though data were sparse.

To start, the DOS indicated in its DEIS (the section on dioxin inhalation) that emission concentrations for dioxin compounds vary only moderately if one focuses on facilities with similar features. Thus, they justified the use of the Martin facilities in Europe and the United States as the total sample for the definition of expected emission rates for the proposed Brooklyn facility. Using standard emission rates from these facilities, the DOS predicted that a maximum ground level concentration of TCDD per year would be only 2.57×10^{-8} micrograms per cubic meter, and a ground level concentration for 2,3,7,8-TCDD per year only

1.68×10^{-9} micrograms per cubic meter (DOS 1984: 2–42). For TCDD, this level was only 27 percent of the Acceptable Ambient Level (AAL) established in the Air Guideline No. 1 by the New York State Department of Environmental Conservation. According to the EPA, any facility achieving such a low emission level of TCDD "would not present a public health hazard for residents living in the immediate vicinity" (DOS 1984: 2–42). Concerned readers were directed to the Hart report to derive the calculations.

But the main pathway of concern according to the DOS was not that of inhalation. Instead, the DOS identified ingestion as the main pathway. Here, the focus was directed toward dioxin compounds that concentrate in soil, street dirt, and house dust. Ingestion was assumed to include various amounts of direct consumption of soil or dust on food and various percentages of bioavailability. Again drawing on the standard deposition rates from incinerators in the narrow sample, a maximum concentration of 0.077×10^{-12} gram per gram of street dirt was predicted for 2,3,7,8-TCDD. This maximum rate of exposure through ingestion and dermal absorption of 2,3,7,8-TCDD was expected to be 2.4 times more than the amount from inhalation alone. Still, the DOS characterized the maximum predicted impacts of concentrations of dioxin compounds in the soil and in street and household dirt to be "extremely low." And in the case of 2,3,7,8-TCDD, for instance, the human intake from ingestion or dermal contact was "insignificant" (DOS 1984: 2–47, 2–48).

A couple of comments are worth making before we move on to evaluate the Hart report. The first is that the DOS never mentioned in the DEIS that cancer of the bladder was associated with exposure to dioxin compounds. This downplayed the extent to which public health was at stake. The second is that by spending only a few pages on the issue of dioxin, most readers probably overlooked the problem altogether.

By comparison, the Hart report appears to be an extremely thorough study of the properties of dioxin compounds, their emission rates, levels of exposure, and exposure risks to humans. Dioxin emission data were selected from the Chicago-Northwest facility and the Zurich-Josefstrasse facility, although data were also compiled from Hampton (Virginia), Sweden, Italy, and the Netherlands (Hart 1984: A–1/A–6). The lowest emissions were observed from the first two incinerators with the same basic design as the proposed facility in Brooklyn. Several orders of magnitude in the emissions test data from the other incinerators demonstrated the wide range of PCDD and emissions. Both gases and particulates of PCDD and PCDF compounds were assessed for ambient exposure levels in areas surrounding the Brooklyn Navy Yard. The actual emissions of the Brooklyn facility would presumably fall somewhere between these levels so that both were used to develop an exposure assessment and risk assessment (Hart 1984: 3–35). The total CDF was, respectively, 82.92 ug/sec. for gaseous emissions and 38.79 ug/sec. for particulate emissions, and the total CDD was, respectively, 9.54 ug/sec. for gaseous emissions and 4.46 ug/sec. for particulate emissions (Hart 1984: 3–36).

To assess ambient air concentrations and downwind concentrations in the soil, street dirt, and house dust, the analysts used a Multiple Point Source Gaussian Dispersion Algorithm with Optional Terrain Adjustment (in cities, MPTERU) computer dispersion, and an Industrial Source Complex (ISC) computer deposition. Both models were developed by the EPA. Each calculates concentrations at several hundred ground-level and elevated locations based on five years of meteorological data. Assuming all PCDF and PCDD emissions were either particulates or gaseous, the Hart group predicted that the maximum annual average concentrations due to emissions would be only 0.9309–1.9900 for PCDF, 0.0882–0.2290 for PCDD, and 0.0008–0.0019 for 2,3,7,8-TCDD, all in pg per cubic meter (Hart 1984: 4–5/4–7). The maximum concentration in the soil would be, respectively, only 0.486, 0.560, and 0.001 pg per gram. And the maximum concentration in street and household dirt would be, respectively, only 104, 12, and 0.087 pg per gram (Hart 1984: 4–19).

Using these estimates of PCDD and PCDF concentrations for all three potential pathways of exposure, the Hart group then performed a risk assessment in order to calculate the range of cancer risk to residents in the Brooklyn area. The assessment compared the predicted ambient air concentrations and estimated daily intake levels for both PCDDs and PCDFs.

The Hart group speculated that the maximum increased cancer risk would range from less than 0.24 to the upper bound limit of less than 5.9×10^{-6} for all pathways combined. The latter estimate was the upper bound of the excess cancer risk in the worst case (Hart 1984: 17). This is quite a minimal risk: only about six chances in a million of initiating cancer.

Despite Hart's careful listing of all the uncertainties in the risk assessment, the choice to rely on precise values for parameters resulted in a precise estimate of health risk at the end. Hart specified that scientific judgment was used to make up for lack of data, uncertain animal-human extrapolations, and worst-case estimates. Still, the reference to a maximum cancer risk of precisely 0.24 to 5.9×10^{-6} communicated a degree of confidence that could only be hopeful at best. If there are significant inadequacies in the data, rough estimates, and assumptions based on weak premises, how can scientific consultants be confident enough to make estimations that are precise to many decimal places?

The LNG Case

By 1976, no court had compelled the FPC to perform a "certain" analysis of health risk. Nevertheless, the FPC *did* produce a precise estimation of the health risk. It used a formal methodology to avoid any challenge of the uncertain data.

The FPC decided to rely on a worst-case sequence model of the risks of a tanker accident leading to human fatalities. The FPC commissioned Science Applications, Inc. to perform the worst-case assessment based on a large-scale spill of LNG from a tanker collision or grounding. Such a model calculates the probability of a human fatality as the product of the conditional probabilities of all intermediate events considered necessary for that fatality to occur:

Risk (fatalities per exposed person per year) $= P1 \times P2 \times P3 \times P4$, where

$P1 =$ Tanker accident rate times the number of trips per year,
$P2 =$ Probability of a spill in the event of a tanker accident,
$P3 =$ Probability of the formations of a vapor cloud and ignition affecting populated areas,
$P4 =$ Probability of fatalities resulting from exposure to the vapor cloud.

The worst case estimate was interpreted to be a spill of only one compartment of a tanker, but not a full tanker (FPC 1976: 3–9). Based on this equation, SAI and FPC calculated that the risk of a tanker accident and worst-case spill of one compartment (immediate ignition causing a vapor cloud) would result in a maximum number of about 2,500 fatalities per year (FPC 1976: App. A, Table 8). The frequency of this ignited vapor cloud was estimated to be only about once every 100,000 years (FPC 1976: App A, Table 6)!

Despite the rareness of this risk, the key public health issue concerned the last parameter—the number of people who might be exposed to a vapor cloud onshore. The key question was how far could the dense gas vapor travel onshore following an LNG spill offshore that did not ignite immediately. This was assumed to be a 10 percent chance, given that immediate ignition of the dense gas vapor was expected. Fatalities due to ignition of the gas could be expected within the area covered by the cloud's plume. SAI chose to model the movement of the vapor cloud as if it were a nondense gas. This was based on the assumption that in a persistent wind, a vapor cloud will move downwind and disperse laterally and vertically. Furthermore, methane was assumed to have a density much less than air, and thus to be a light gas (FPC 1976: 41, 45, Appendix A).

In its Final Environmental Impact Statement, therefore, the FPC's models (based on the SAI Report) showed that the LNG plume could rapidly dilute in the presence of a 5 mph wind (FPC 1976: A–44). The wind was assumed to blow in all directions. The cloud was thus expected to travel only a short distance to the farthest point of possible ignition, the lower flammable limit (LFL). Any ignition up to this LFL would burn back to the spill site, causing fatalities equal to the population in that area swept by the cloud. Beyond this LFL limit, the concentration of the LNG vapor would be insufficient to ignite and burn. The FEIS predicted 1.2–2.82 km as the maximum distance to the LFL for a 25,000–100,000 m3 LNG spill. SAI, however, estimated that a 37,500 m3 spill could travel downwind from 1–6 km, depending upon the windspeed (FPC 1976: Attachment A, Table 4; 3–10, 3–23).

The FPC did reveal the assumptions that other scientists used to account for their varying estimates of plume travel predictions. These included the use of a gravity spread model and the incorporation of positive buoyancy into the dispersion model. Different assumptions were also made about atmospheric stability, different windspeeds, and dispersion based on point-source, line-source, or area-source.

Still, precise risk estimates resulted from use of the precise methodology: the conditional probability accident model. This precision was much greater than was even required by NEPA. Why were such apparently certain risks challenged in the LNG and dioxin cases? And why did the conservative estimate in the saccharin case, ranging over three orders of magnitude, fare no better?

SCIENTIFIC CONTROVERSY

Despite diverse statutory requirements and risk assessments, all three regulatory agencies faced challenges from critical scientists. The scientific evidence was too fragmentary and inconclusive to avoid alternative interpretations. This section therefore reviews the adversarial institutional settings, varying roles of scientists, and varying aspects of risk that contributed to controversies. It primarily emphasizes the diverse types of scientific uncertainty that constituted the challenges. We will use the controversies in the three case studies to demonstrate each of these issues.

Institutional Settings

Agency and nonagency scientists are drawn into institutional hearings to report on how well their own scientific findings support the proposed agency decision. In this way, they play roles as expert witnesses in either administrative hearings of the regulatory agency, public hearings required by NEPA and state law, legislative hearings by Senate or House committees or subcommittees, or judicial hearings in civil court. These increasingly adversarial forums pit the agency against citizens and then against other bodies of the government. Congress's intention through the Administrative Procedures Act was to govern how administrative agencies ought to function. Ever since the passage of this law in 1946, most statutes specify that agencies can be challenged by lawsuits of opponents. In this way, agency decisions must be checked against the ruling of an administrative judge. Generally this is a cooperative review of the scientific evidence supporting the proposed decision. In the LNG case, for instance, one administrative judge even denied the scientific validity of an expert's critical testimony.

More adversarial are the public hearings specified by NEPA, which pit agencies against the public regarding the safety of a proposed decision. According to their statutes, the regulatory directives of the EPA and state environmental agencies are to conduct hearings during which any member of the public can voice opinions and critique proposed decisions. During periods of public comment, the discussions are frequently controversial. In the LNG case, however, the residents of Everett were so unconcerned about the proposed expansion of the LNG terminal that only a very few arrived to protest the decision.

When citizens are opposed to a decision by an agency, they can request that Congress take up their plea. The investigation of the scientific basis for a regulatory decision can be performed by either a committee or subcommittee of the Senate or the House of Representatives. In Chapter 4 we see how aptly Senate and House subcommittees examined the proposed saccharin decision and used uncertain scientific evidence to build a consensus among the scientists that a different decision would also be acceptable.

The most adversarial forum is usually a hearing by citizens in civil court. Congress has facilitated this critical role of citizens by specifying in agency statutes that citizens can file lawsuits directly against an

offending party, like a regulatory agency, for not performing its statutory
mandate properly. This usually occurs when an agency has failed to act,
although the specification can vary from statute to statute. This is
commonly called a citizen suit provision.

Such adversarial institutional settings would be less of a problem for
regulatory agencies if all scientists viewed health risks in the same way.
If so, proposed decisions would be much less vulnerable. The problem
is that scientists *do* have conflicting perspectives that can be exacerbated
by adversarial settings.

Roles of Scientists

The role of scientists in most environmental decisions breaks into that
of professional, ideologue, or consultant. A professional is a scientist
who is committed to the scientific discovery of objective truth without
preselected goals of research. Research is rational, impartial, open to
counterexample, and protected from nonscientific judgment. Serge Taylor (1984: 22–23) outlines five features in the sociology and philosophy
of science that explain the coherence and integrity of professional
scientists:

1. Norms: disagreements are decided on the basis of empirical, logical,
   and analytic grounds.
2. Impartial behavior: proponents of a theory cannot monopolize resources in order to protect the theory from being invalidated.
3. Suspended judgment: freedom exists to suspend judgment on a
   disputed problem until new empirical data can reveal the truth.
4. Social reward: scientists are encouraged to detect errors in the research
   of others.
5. Insulation: scientists are not subject to the norms or values of other
   professions.

For example, extensive animal and human research has tried to
understand whether it is a molecular or threshold dynamic of irreversible
damage to DNA that leads to the incidence of cancer. Still, no definitive
judgment has yet been made by professional scientists about the process
through which chemicals are processed in the body. The irreversible
damage may be based on a single insult ("hit"), multiple hits, a dose rate
that defines the number of stages, immunological responses, or other
biological mechanisms that can cause a carcinogen and other processes

in the body to interact. We shall see that the scientists in both the saccharin and LNG cases participated as professionals.

A second role that scientists can play is important because it directs the outcome of research, although not the process. This role is ideological. Ideological scientists are more committed to preserving the environment and people's lives politically than they are to carrying out the process of scientific discovery or technological innovation. They do not distrust science, but they do distrust its use unselectively for any social purpose. Edith Efron (1984:57) believes that such "apocalyptic" scientists use "vacant abstractions, arbitrary extrapolations, conclusions based on inadequate or nonexistent data; the rejection of logic; and the incorporation of moral attitudes into the very 'core' of their 'scientific' thought." As apocalyptic scientists she includes Barry Commoner, Thomas Corbett, Samuel Epstein, and others.

I take a more modest approach. The application of science to different ends, even if political, is analogous to the application of science when consulting. The public is never deceived by either ideological scientists or consulting scientists because their political values are always explicit.

The final role of many scientists is as consultants. Similar to ideological scientists, consultants follow scientific methods but have preselected goals of research. These goals are generally provided by the client— whether industrial company, government agency, or citizen group. The scientist is obliged to develop research findings that support the client's goal, particularly if the scientist hopes to be hired again or wants to develop a good reputation in correlating research findings with client goals. Often clients want risk levels to be either extremely low or extremely high. This polarity makes it easier for the client to argue for or against a restrictive decision.

We shall see that both Commoner and Hart acted as consultants to the Brooklyn residents and the DOS, respectively. Commoner volunteered his services, while Hart was hired directly. Both consultants, however, developed research findings that supported only their respective clients' goals of proposing or opposing the incinerator. Although Fay and the scientists in the LNG case acted as professionals, their findings were presented only as supportive or opposing evidence. Not only did scientists take different roles and appear in different types of adversarial hearings, but they also disagreed with one another over how to estimate risk.

Risks

Scientists disagree on which pathway of exposure leads to the worst risk. One scientist may claim that inhalation of dioxin is the most dangerous intake, while another might insist that consumption of dioxin on the food we eat is the worst intake.

The most critical disagreements between scientists occur over the level of risk. The level of risk indicates how bad the hazard is expected to be. It is usually stated as the rate of individual risk: the ratio of the number of excess deaths from the hazard divided by the total number of people in the exposed population. This is often expressed for the 70-year period of a lifetime. Thus, the maximum (worst-case) individual rate of risk in the dioxin case was six excess cancer deaths per million people exposed over a lifetime, according to Hart's calculations. But according to Commoner's calculations, the worst-case rate of risk was substantially larger. The highest credible risk level is about what people care, and the greater the range of uncertainty about that level, the more credible it is that the risk is high.

Scientists also frequently disagree about the number of people exposed. In the LNG case we shall see how the agency's scientist and the nonagency scientist differed by a factor of ten in their estimates of the size of the exposed population. When the interpretive models or theories of a scientist are based upon insufficient research data, he or she must be ready for scientific challenges.

Types of Scientific Uncertainty

Differences in risk estimates establish the potential for scientific disagreement. But how can we understand this nature of scientific challenges? We must look in more detail at the kinds of scientific uncertainty that are involved. Here we propose four types of uncertainty that were critical in the three primary case studies: data, extrapolation, model, and parametric uncertainties.

Data uncertainty occurs when scientists disagree about what data to use to analyze a risk. Generally, uncertainties over data include insufficient numbers of studies, different types of samples, or apparently contradictory findings. In the saccharin case, for example, there was no controlled epidemiological study up to 1976 of the carcinogenic effect of saccharin in humans. Data were therefore extremely uncertain, if existent at all.

Extrapolation uncertainty is when scientists disagree over whether it is possible to quantify animal findings to make judgments about human risk. This was the primary issue of disagreement in the saccharin case. Many scientists were not willing to agree on precise numbers of people at cancer risk judging from animal evidence.

Another type of uncertainty concerns the *model* of human health risk. Scientists may disagree over different parameters that should be included in models of human health risk. The fundamental disagreement between the SAI and Fay in the LNG case, for instance, was over whether wind speed or atmospheric turbulence should be the basis for estimating the distance traveled by the vapor cloud.

The final type of uncertainty is *parametric*. This occurs when scientists disagree over how to estimate the same parameter. In the dioxin case, for example, Hart and Commoner disagreed sharply over whether the worst-case estimate for the emissions rate of dioxin should be the low value existing at the Chicago Northwest incinerator or the high value reported at the Hampton incinerator.

The following case studies of the saccharin, dioxin, and LNG decisions demonstrate how scientists used these four types of uncertainty to challenge the risk estimates of the scientists working for the agencies. The cases also show the play of diverse institutional contexts and roles of scientists.

The Saccharin Case. Professional scientists supportive of the FDA relied on existing animal data and extrapolation methods to justify the agency's estimation of carcinogenic risk. Although a carcinogenic effect was unlikely, the probability was high of being exposed to cancer through diet drinks or other sources of saccharin in the U.S. population. Opposing professional scientists insisted that the research uncertainties on saccharin were too great. Epidemiological data were insufficient, and the quantification of the extrapolation from rat tests to human risks was questionable. Such uncertainties might even undermine the initial claim that saccharin was a human carcinogen at all.

Here we look at the Senate's hearings on the risks of saccharin use and at the ban proposed by the FDA. In 1973 the National Academy of Sciences critically examined the studies by the Wisconsin Alumni Research Foundation and the FDA. Although the NAS did agree that the studies showed cancer rates in animals apparently associated with high levels of consumption of saccharin, it decided at that early stage that saccharin could not be blamed for human risk when the data correlating rat with human responses were still insufficient.

In March 1977 Congress decided to act. By June the Subcommittee on Health and Scientific Research of the Committee on Human Resources of the U.S. Senate called a hearing to examine the risks of using saccharin and the decision by the FDA to ban the chemical additive from the market (Subcommittee on Health and Scientific Research 1977). The intention of the hearing was to raise scientific arguments for and against the decision that saccharin was a carcinogen in animals as well as humans.

One of the first reports in the hearing was a study performed by a panel of medical scientists assisting the staff of the Office of Technology Assessment, which had been requested by the Subcommittee of the Senate. The panel concluded that saccharin was a carcinogen in animals, and was therefore also a potential cause of cancer in humans. But the panel stressed that the method of extrapolating from positive animal evidence to human risk was not valid. Quantitative extrapolations would "not currently permit reliable estimates of the numbers or locations of cancers that might occur in humans" (testimony of Robbins, Subcommittee on Health and Scientific Research 1977: 53). Finally, the panel stated that existing epidemiological studies of humans were insufficient to determine whether saccharin was actually a carcinogen when ingested by humans. The panel therefore concluded that the FDA scientists were optimistic in presuming that extrapolation was quantitatively valid and that epidemiological data were sufficient for saccharin to be considered carcinogenic in humans.

The key types of scientific uncertainty that were raised during the hearing were both extrapolation and data. One uncertainty regarded the validity of the quantitative extrapolation from rat tests to human risk. The best presentation of the argument favoring extrapolation is Dr. Joyce McCann's during the Senate hearing (testimony of McCann, Subcommittee on Health and Scientific Research 1977: 64–67). She made four points: (1) rat cancer tests used validly high doses, (2) these tests indicated that saccharin is a weak carcinogen in rats, (3) saccharin is likely to be a weak carcinogen in people, and (4) though weak, it poses a significant health hazard to humans.

First, she justified the use of a high dose by pointing out that the higher the dose, the more that exposed people or rats get cancer. To test low doses would require several thousands of rats to see what the equivalent results would be in humans. The extremely high dose of saccharin, an amount equivalent to 800 diet drinks a day, is reasonable if the researcher wants to use only 100 rats in an experiment. This will result in at least 10 percent of the rats initiating cancer if saccharin is a carcinogen. Her second point differentiated the potencies of various kinds of carcinogens of saccharin (Ibid: 65).

But McCann's third point concerned a data uncertainty. Scientists had roughly correlated carcinogenic potency in rats with that in humans. The human evidence, however, was fragmentary. Given that epidemiologists cannot do controlled experiments on people, the only evidence in 1975 was six cases of actual cancer incidence from doses of saccharin. In these cases the potency of the carcinogen in animals and people was roughly correlated. Because the biological potencies of carcinogens can range over a factor of a million, McCann argued that this rough correlation was "quite significant" (Ibid: 66). Thus she claimed that the rat cancer data allowed scientists to predict that saccharin would be a weak carcinogen in people. And given that so many people consume saccharin in substantial amounts, McCann claimed, in her fourth point, that scientists could estimate risk estimates "ranging up to several thousand expected new cases of cancer each year" (Ibid). She noted, however, that these estimates could vary by a factor of 10 to 100 hundred due to uncertainties in the extrapolation. One difficulty in this third part of the argument, however, was the use of only one small epidemiological study to justify a correlation between potencies of rat and human carcinogens.

Evidence from a postdecision study of saccharin done by the National Research Council of the NAS (NRC 1978) concluded, instead, that epidemiological studies of the relationship between saccharin and bladder cancer appeared to be negative. Moreover, time-trend studies provided no indication of an association between saccharin and bladder cancer, although the effects of synergistic factors like cigarette smoking are difficult to separate out (Armstrong and Doll 1975). Studies on diabetics also never show a positive association between saccharin use and bladder cancer, although the special characteristics of this population are difficult to use in extrapolations to the public (Armstrong et al. 1976; Armstrong and Doll 1975). Nor do case-control studies offer positive evidence either to support or refute the association between saccharin use and bladder cancer (Kessler and Clark 1978). The first case supported the finding that the proportion of male bladder cancer patients using artificial sweeteners was higher than the proportion of male controls who did not. But the second case supported a contrary finding: no excess cases of bladder cancer could be attributed to the use of saccharin. We will discuss the problem of such contrary findings on saccharin in Chapter 4 (see also NRC 1978: 3-103).

Even uncertainties about saccharin's behavior as a typical carcinogen raise doubts about human risk. The focus here is on the metabolic, mutagenic, and hormonal responses of rats, rather than humans, to saccharin. Most substances that induce cancer become carcinogens only after they have been transformed by the body into active metabolites. The typical mechanism for inducing cancer is direct action on the DNA. This was not true of saccharin in animal tests. Saccharin does not appear to cause any action on the DNA. Moreover, doses in rats were vastly greater than realistic equivalents in humans. These high doses suggested, therefore, that carcinogenic effects might occur only under extreme laboratory conditions of overexposure to saccharin. Given such uncertainties about saccharin's effect on rats, any extrapolation to humans was highly questionable (Burns 1977: 60–61).

The case shows that both data and extrapolation uncertainties were fundamental to the dispute among professional scientists over saccharin consumption. This review, however, covers only the dispute that transpired in the Senate's hearing. The general debate over saccharin risk focused on the probability of cancer and the number of people exposed. The dioxin example, by contrast, shows that uncertainties of parametric estimation could also be important.

The Dioxin Case. In this case the critical consultant, Commoner, relied mostly on parameter and data uncertainties to criticize the carcinogenic risk estimated by Hart and the DOS. This was because the models of all three scientific consultants were much more similar than were those of divergent scientists in the saccharin case. Nonetheless, the range of scientific uncertainty in the dioxin case spanned from a high to a low level of risk.

The controversy between scientists in the dioxin case emerged through reports favoring and challenging the DOS's preliminary environmental impact statement. This was consistent with SEQRA's requirements that criticism and response occur before or during public hearings on the agency's EIS. Commoner et al. (1984) published his *Environmental and Economic Analysis of Alternative Municipal Solid Waste Disposal Technologies* in order to criticize the Department of Sanitation's preliminary version of its EIS. In response, the DOS hired the John Hart Company in 1984 to do a public health assessment specifically of the dioxin risk (Hart 1984). These two reports were the first indication that scientists disagreed strongly over the level of health risk. This level of risk was due to exposure to dioxin in the ambient air surrounding the municipal waste incinerator.

Commoner et al. (1984) challenged the DOS's estimate of cancer risk from emissions of the municipal waste incinerator. Hart had estimated a maximum level of risk at only six cases of cancer per million people exposed to the dioxin emissions over a lifetime. Commoner's report justified a much greater risk. Commoner et al. (1984:17) calculated that the risk could instead be 1,430 excess cases of cancer per million people exposed to the same emissions. This latter estimate represents a very high lifetime cancer risk of over one in a thousand chances.

A central theoretical disagreement between two scientific consultants was whether dioxin compounds are formed in the combustion chamber or in the stack. Hart, the scientific consultant hired by the DOS, considered three theories of dioxin (PCDD/PCDF) formation. All of these examined the formation of dioxin as a parameter inside the combustion chamber. First, trace components of dioxin compounds could be present in the refuse to be incinerated. In normal municipal waste the amount would be negligible. Second, dioxin compounds could be produced from precursors such as polychlorinated byphenols (PCBs). Finally dioxin compounds could be newly formed from materials unrelated to dioxin compounds, such as plastics or petroleum products. In the latter case, reactions between decomposed products of organic compounds and chlorine would create PCDDs or PCDFs when heated (DOS 1985: D-11.9, 11.10). Hart considered that precursors and new sources would be both produced and destroyed at the established temperature of the combustion chamber (Hart 1984: 3–2).

But Commoner, the biologist hired by Brooklyn neighborhood groups, had a different theory about the location where dioxin was formed. He contended that the adsorption of dioxin precursors to fly ash particles occurred in the stack or control device, *not* in the combustion chamber. Such precursors come from lignin in paper or from chlorine, a combustion product of polyvinylchloride plastic and salt. Referring to the study by Buser et al. (1978), Commoner pointed out that only a negligible amount of a single congener was found on fly ash in the combustion chamber. This suggested that little PCDD or PCDF would be produced or destroyed under high temperature in the combustion chamber. But significant amounts of all expected congeners were found in the stack (Commoner 1984: 27–28). This evidence suggested that the parameter of dioxin formation was in the PCDFs and PCDDs that were formed in the stack *after* combustion.

A similar lack of common theory and conclusive evidence caused disagreement between the consultants over the parameter for the temperature at which dioxin compounds are formed or destroyed. In its FEIS the DOS (1985), cited evidence that temperatures between 590–750 degrees centigrade in the combustion chamber are likely to produce dioxin compounds. For instance, 750°C was cited as optimal for PCDD production by the herbicide 2,4,5-T and related compounds. Pyrolysis also converts chlorobenzenes to dioxin compounds through terminal oxidation at 620°C. Finally, evidence showed that dioxin is formed by the combustion of lignosulfonate pulp paste at 590°C in the presence of hydrochloric acid. Lignin and a chlorine donor combine (DOS 1985: D-11.10, 11.11). Based on this evidence, the consultant to the DOS claimed that over 99 percent of PCDDs and PCDFs would be destroyed at temperatures between 700–957°C in the combustion chamber (Hart 1984: 3–3/3–8).

But Commoner opposed this viewpoint based on his understanding that the temperature in the stack, not in the combustion chamber, was the critical parameter to dioxin formation. He argued that the critical temperatures for dioxin formation were below 200–400°C. Since adsorption does not occur above 400°C he insisted that dioxin formation must occur in parts of the incineration system such as the stack that are *below* that temperature. Furthermore, the reaction adding chlorine to precursor molecules absorbed on fly ash is maximum at 200°C or lower. Again, this would be found in the stack or in other cooler parts of the incineration system (Commoner 1984: 27, 29). Thus, the two scientists advocated different evidence of parameters to justify opposing views about temperature.

In choosing representative incinerators, both scientists were also confronted by uncertainties regarding data. If the furnace temperature was of concern, then the Hampton facility was about 121–218°C higher than the 650°C temperature of the Chicago facility. Hampton was therefore much closer to the 980°C design temperature of the Brooklyn facility. This would accommodate the conventional theory that PCDD and PCDF compounds are destroyed in the furnace if the combustion temperature is sufficiently high (a minimum of one to two seconds of gas residence time at a combustion temperature of 900–1000°C (Hart 1984: 7–8).

Commoner was not convinced, however, that the furnace was the key site where dioxin is both formed and destroyed. Evidence showed that the Hampton facility, with an EPA-tested (1984) furnace temperature of only 771–868°C, had an emission rate of PCDD and PCDF as high as 50 times that of the Chicago facility. This high dioxin emissions rate, despite a high furnace temperature, meant that dioxin destruction was more evasive than supposed (Commoner et al. 1984).

Commoner therefore looked at a broad range of emissions rates among the seven facilities, with Chicago being the lowest [180 ng/m^3 (1983)] and Hampton, Virginia, being the highest [12,620 ng/m^3 (1983) and

10,355 ng/m³ (1984)]. Commoner chose the highest rate at Hampton in order to estimate his cancer risk in the worst case. Actual EPA measurements at the Hampton facility over a five-day period in 1984 showed an extremely wide range of emission rates for PCDDs and PCDFs—between 4,790 and 26,500 ng/m³, owing to a fluctuation of only 799–868°C in the furnace temperature (EPA 1984b).

But instead of using a high emission rate for his worst-case value, Hart chose a relatively low value of 180 ng/m³ from his sample of data from eight incinerators (Hart 1984: 3–38). This he justified because a similarly designed facility in Chicago reported a low emission rate. The Chicago-Northwest incinerator had a similar Martin furnace design, waste type, and dioxin sampling method as would be used in the proposed Brooklyn incinerator. Hart argued that these similarities justified his choice of the relatively low dioxin emission rate to simulate probable conditions at the Brooklyn site.

We have pointed out that the worst-case estimates of excess cancer risk of the two consultants differed by over two orders of magnitude. This was largely due to the discrepancy in choices of dioxin emission rates. Hart's rate would result in an exposure of only 28.2 percent of the Air Guideline set by the New York State Department of Environmental Conservation for maximum exposure. Commoner et al., however, reported that at his high worst-case emission rate, the guideline would be overshot by 905 percent. Similarly, Hart's low emission rate would result in an exposure level that was only 2.9 percent of that allowed by the New York State Department of Health. Commoner's, by contrast, would result in an exposure level that was 109 percent of the maximum allowed (Hart 1984: 5–52; Commoner et al. 1984: Table VI).

Scientific consultants caused heated debate by focusing on varying parameters of location, temperature, and dioxin emission rate. The scientific uncertainties at stake pushed Commoner's level of risk up to one chance in a thousand of initiating cancer. Although more uncertain, the disagreement among scientists in the LNG case was much less vociferous.

The LNG Case. The criticism of the professional consultant to the Federal Power Commission in the LNG case focused primarily on model uncertainties. Scientists disagreed on which of several parameters should estimate the distance traveled by the accidentally released vapor cloud. This parameter would determine the number of people exposed to the risk.

A public hearing was called by the administrative judge who oversaw the FPC's environmental impact statement. This hearing occurred first in Everett, Massachusetts, and later in Washington, D.C., for the local and federal examinations of the proposed expansion of the terminal.

Professor James Fay, a cryogenic specialist at Massachusetts Institute of Technology (MIT), led the scientific opposition. Fay's purpose was to criticize the assumptions and models used by the scientists at SAI assisted by the staff of the FPC. He disagreed that the risk to lives would be quite small. Technically, the actual safety risk was defined as the point at which an individual would be burned or thermally radiated to the point of death from exposure to a vapor cloud of LNG that had ignited. The FPC had calculated that the probability of a worst-case spill of one compartment of the tanker, immediately ignited, would be only about one in 10 million chances of fatality per exposed person per year (FPC 1976: 3–11).

But Fay insisted that the risk would be more severe. He focused instead on the consequences of risk rather than on the probability. First, he denied that the number of fatalities from an ignited vapor cloud would be only 2,000 to 3,000 in the worst case. Fay insisted, instead, that the number could be nearly 20,000 people in Everett, Chelsea, East Boston, and other cities bordering the Boston Harbor (Fay 1976: 36). Although Fay's number of people affected seems unacceptable, technically it is only a one-order-of-magnitude difference from the number presented by the FPC.

Instead of stating his risk in probabilistic terms, Fay used the more compelling "number of deaths" to convince decisionmakers of the unacceptable risk at stake. Baruch Fischhoff (1985: 89) has emphasized how politically strategic is such a choice of how to define risk.

Despite these worst-case risk estimates, the focus of another aspect of the controversy was not on immediate ignition but on whether wind speed (SAI) or atmospheric turbulence (Fay) would be the critical parameter needed to determine the distance traveled by the LNG vapor cloud. This distance at which the vapor cloud is no longer flammable is called the lower flammable limit. The LFL determines the geographic area over which people could be at risk in a situation that is worst-case.

This controversy represents a model uncertainty. The analyses of scientists and staff focused on whether or not a positive decision should be made to expand the LNG terminal. The analysis of the FPC and SAI was that the decision should be positive because the probability of risk was low. Fay, however, believed that the decision should be negative, because the number of potential fatalities was unacceptably high. Let us start from the agreement between the two scientific perspectives and then show where the critical disagreement emerged.

The FPC staff and their consultant, the SAI company, agreed with Professor Fay that dense LNG gas clouds spread from negative to neutral buoyancy, at which point they are no longer ignitable. Once an LNG spill from a tanker occurred, the liquid would evaporate to form a negatively buoyant cloud of dense gas. Different from the diffusion of other pollutants such as dioxin, this cloud would roll along the water or ground because its molecular weight is greater than that of air. But as the cloud gained heat from the water and· surrounding air, it would expand from negative to neutral buoyancy. At that point, its density would be the same as the air. It would shift from a primary mechanism of gravitational spreading to one of atmospheric diffusion (Fay and Zamba 1986: 3-4; FPC 1976: Att. 36,37).

What the consultants did not agree on, however, was whether wind speed or turbulence was the critical parameter needed to disperse the cloud to its lower flammable limit. The FPC staff, advised by their consultant, assumed that wind velocity was critical. Once gravitational spreading was less than the local wind speed (i.e., neutral buoyancy), the cloud would move in the direction of the wind. The distance traveled would be equal to the wind speed multiplied by the time period under consideration. The consultants assumed that the wind speed would be 5 mph, the velocity expected to give the longest cloud plumes. They also assumed that any direction would be equally probable. Theoretically, lower speeds would produce even longer plumes, although such speeds would also be more susceptible to variability in wind direction. Similarly, stronger winds would disperse clouds more rapidly, reducing fire hazards downwind. The downwind distance of the LFL would be reached when the concentration of methane vapor was 5 percent of the air in the cloud (FPC 1976: 36-45).

But Fay, the cryogenic expert, disagreed strongly with this analysis of the wind parameter in two main ways. First, he claimed that dense gas clouds such as LNG *decrease* rather than increase their rate of dilution in the presence of wind. This differs from nondense gases (Fay Comments, FPC 1976: 41-42). This claim emphasizes the dominant role of gravitational motion in preserving the integrity of the cloud volume rather than of the wind in eroding it. When the dense gas falls to the ground, it spreads horizontally more than vertically. This was not assumed in the FPC's FEIS. Second, he claimed that it was the shear in the wind field, or "turbulence," rather than the wind velocity that explained the rate of dilution. Theoretically, this determined the LFL. A turbulent mixing of the plume and surrounding air would be generated by shear in the atmospheric wind field. This involves both horizontal and vertical mixing of the plume. Later in 1986, Fay explained that because dense gas plumes tend not to grow in height, they remain within a region of the atmospheric boundary layer whose characteristic velocity is the "friction velocity." The rate of vertical mixing of the plume within this atmospheric layer determines the distance traveled. Eventually "passive" dispersion replaces negative buoyancy as the mixing agent (Fay and Zamba 1986: 2–4).

This discrepancy primarily explains the differences between Fay's and the FPC's models of vapor cloud travel to the lower flammable limit. Fay predicted that the LFL would be theoretically as far as 9 km in neutral atmospheric conditions and 58 km in very stable conditions. Practically, he suggested, however, that the vapor cloud would probably ignite sooner, within a worst-case boundary of 4 km on either side of the Boston ship channel (Fay comments, FPC 1976). This case demonstrates how important model uncertainties are. These uncertainties could determine how many people would be harmed if a vapor cloud ignited.

SUMMARY

All four types of scientific uncertainty turned out to be controversial in the cases. Disputes over different types of scientific uncertainties became intractable for scientists to resolve because of uncertain data, extrapolation, models, and parameters. Scientists ended up playing different roles in unexpectedly adversarial settings. Brooks and Cooper's (1987) scientific unknowns and "contextual ignorances" proliferated. Regulators remained disconcerted, as Graham et al. (1989) claim, about whether scientific research would ever produce scientific knowledge that could foster regulation. It may be that health science is simply too young and subjective when compared to the more mature and objective physical sciences (Morgan et al. 1984). Whatever the reason, politics is still free to play the cards of scientific inquiry with its own rules.

Chapter 3 focuses on the opposition that citizens launched against agency decisions. Were citizens concerned about these statutory requirements, risk assessments, or scientific controversies? Or, did they have their own mechanisms of grassroots protest?

Chapter Three

Bargains with Citizens

Citizens use uncertain science provided by scientists to raise doubts about agency expertise and competence. Science thus becomes partial, and the process of controversy shapes public opinion and extracts concessions from agencies. I analyze controversy as a bargaining process between agencies and citizens in which scientists hold the key resource of scientific influence: uncertainty about evidence.

I draw from the work of Dorothy Nelkin (1979: 191) and Harvey Sapolsky (1986), who study the changing role of experts in controversies. Nelkin points out that the role of experts has shifted from one of authority based on expertise to one of politician based on partial information. Up to the 1960s, scientists generally relied on their ability to collect and rationalize scientific data as the basis for undisputed authority. But during the period 1960–80, the role of scientists became more ambivalent (Nelkin 1979; Nelkin and Pollack 1981). Scientists tried to increase their credibility by lending expertise to citizens who struggled politically. The unintended consequence of this, however, was that uncertainties in scientific data and interpretation were exposed. Scientists began to fear that they were losing rather than gaining credibility. Citizens began to doubt whether the knowledge of scientists was ever incontrovertible. Could the pursuit of science be an independent and neutral or, instead, just a highly political task (Nelkin 1979: 15–16; Nelkin and Pollack 1981: 100)?

According to Nelkin, the power of controversy now belongs to those who can manipulate knowledge, challenge evidence, and exploit expertise. Expertise on both sides of a controversy focuses on the technical ambiguities and on the inability to predict and control events. This exacerbates conflict among groups. Moreover, since the mass media are drawn to inconsistencies, they report conflicting expertise as news (Nelkin 1987). Knowledge becomes used, according to Nelkin, selectively as a weapon (Nelkin 1979: 15–16). My own argument in this book grows out of this thesis. I contend, however, that the strategic use of scientific uncertainties enables citizens and scientists to create new possibilities for bargaining concessions.

Regulatory agencies and public interest groups also have their own hidden goals. Harvey Sapolsky argues in *Consuming Fears* (1986) that survival needs of some organizations cause them to exaggerate product risks in order to draw public attention. The price to citizens is that regulatory agencies are not consistent. Policies on health risks vacillate as agencies try to respond to every fear of citizens. Moreover, these agencies become torn administratively as they try to meet contradictory goals: absolute protection and freedom of choice. They constantly try to defend themselves against discoveries in science that counter current regulations. Public interest groups can be even more self-interested. They tend to choose risks according to their attractiveness to citizens, qualities such as "champion" risks, or fund-raising potential. The attention of the mass media becomes a critical way to promote interest groups in the public eye (Sapolsky 1986: 17–18, 183–191).

The most attractive goal for citizens, public interest groups, and agencies is still safety. This is the focus of nearly all controversies over proposed agency regulations. But safety has come to mean health risk that can be avoided. Citizens insist on zero risk from exposure to dioxin. Agencies continue to advocate some risk in order to provide benefits for a broader group of citizens. Or, the tables reverse and citizens want the risks of saccharin, but agencies refuse to allow them. Thus, despite a common goal of safety, neither citizens nor agencies find an easy compromise on risk taking.

According to Aaron Wildavsky (1988: 3–4), however, the common aim should be to achieve more safety while still taking risks. This is based on his definition of safety as the gain in health relative to the loss in harm from taking a risk. An example would be the health gain from weight loss from the risk of consuming saccharin. Consequently, safety cannot be pursued without a careful assessment by scientists of both the probable gains in health and losses from harm.

However defined, citizens have been particularly critical of agency efforts to site undesirable facilities like industrial plants, waste disposal areas, and prisons. Such protest have become so familiar that decisionmakers call them NIMBYs (Not In My Backyard) or LULUs (Locally Undesirable Land Uses). Citizens staunchly reject municipal waste sites in New York, California, and Pennsylvania; LNG terminals in Massachusetts and Southern California; and nuclear waste disposal areas in Michigan, California, and New Hampshire.

This chapter compares citizen responses to agency decisions to expand the LNG terminal in Everett, Massachusetts, and to site a municipal waste incinerator in Brooklyn, New York. Why did these decisions have such opposed responses? Citizens accepted health risks and neglected scientific information in the first, and rejected risks and worked closely with scientists in the second.

I induce that a bargaining framework begins when agencies negotiate with citizens (Klapp 1989). But the key actor in the early stage of bargaining is the scientific expert. I start the chapter with the LNG case, which is followed by an analysis of bargaining based on certain information. This is contrasted by the dioxin case, which is followed by an analysis of bargaining based on uncertain information. The remainder of the chapter is concerned with bargaining theory, including an introduction to my bargaining model, the Bureaucratic Bargain.

THE LNG CASE

The LNG case was an FPC decision immediately accepted by residents of Everett. This was despite a significant national opposition to the building of other LNG terminals. It was also despite the strong appeal of the cryogenics specialist from MIT, James Fay, who tried to convince residents that the population at risk was much larger than that proposed by the agency.

Cabot Corporation (with foreign investments in oil, gas and minerals) created a subsidiary, Distrigas Corporation, in order to import liquefied natural gas from Skikda, Algeria. Distrigas signed a long-term supply contract (20 years) in 1969 with Algeria's state-owned oil company, the Société Nationale pour la Recherche, la Production, le Transport, la Transformation, et la Commercialization des Hydrocarbures (Sonatrach). The LNG would be imported into Boston Harbor through the terminal in Everett. Algeria retained ownership of the gas up to the flange at the terminal. This gas shipment represented only a small percent (1–1.15) of the total U.S. gas supply up to 1980 (International Petroleum Encyclopedia 1982: 86).

In 1970 the Distrigas Corporation then applied to the City of Everett to approve the construction of two out of four tanks for storage of the LNG. A public hearing occurred at which no opposition was voiced by Everett citizens, and the city's building permit was issued thereafter. Nor did the citizens object when the Massachusetts Department of Public Utilities (DPU) authorized the storage and transport of the LNG in the two public hearings in 1971. Other authorizations were also issued by the Massachusetts Department of Public Safety, the Department of Public Works, the U.S. Coast Guard, and the Everett Fire Department (FPC 1976:1–1).

Neither the state's DPU nor the city's Board of Aldermen were prepared to assess the health risk of these proposed gas tanks. The DPU had to rely on applicants for permits to determine whether proposed operations would be safe. The agency had neither the financial capacity nor the technical information to question company assessment of risk (Corwin interview, 6/4/87). The Board of Aldermen of the Everett city government was no better prepared to assess risk analyses. It assumed that the state DPU would stop any proposed gas tanks if dangerous to Everett residents. Besides, officials of the state and city understood neither how to produce liquefied natural gas nor what safety risks it entailed for residents (McCarthy interview, 6/5/87).

When the importing company, Distrigas, requested permits in 1973 to engage in interstate commerce within the Northeast and Mid-Atlantic, the FPC claimed federal jurisdiction over the terminal. The FPC ordered Distrigas to file an application under Section 7 of the Natural Gas Act to construct and operate the terminal at Everett. But according to NEPA legislation, the FPC also had to conduct an environmental impact assessment, and to convene a public hearing in Boston (October 8, 1976). The purpose was to review potential environmental and health impacts of the terminal expansion and existing safety precautions. The FPC did not expect to run into any challenges of the scientific evidence. Even if there were challenges, NEPA had been reinterpreted by the courts to accept scientific disagreement without requiring that decisions also be altered. A second public hearing also occurred during 1976–77 in Washington, D.C., consistent with procedural rules of the FPC.

By limiting its jurisdiction to only the *offshore* transport of LNG, the FPC avoided the much greater safety and environmental risks of trans-shipment, storage, and transport of the gas onshore. This responsibility was left to the Department of Transportation as part of a separate decision.

Most Everett residents had little reaction to the proposal of the FPC to expand the LNG terminal to include interstate commerce. They also did not comprehend why the transport and transshipment of LNG should be a safety risk for them. The FPC had estimated that a worst-case accident was only about one chance in 10 million, so why should residents be concerned at all? Or, did they forget the other part of the equation: the consequences of a disaster in which about 2,500 citizens from Everett and other cities nearby might die?

Moreover, Everett residents trusted that their aldermen, the DPU, and the FPC would not approve an LNG terminal and operations that were dangerous. Danger, however, was a difficult term to define. Residents of Everett already lived with health risks much greater than any LNG transport or storage. Everett was the site of Exxon's 18 million gallon propane tank. Ignition of this tank could cause a much worse disaster in human fatalities than would the ignition of an LNG vapor cloud (McCarthy interview, 6/5/87). Moreover, during World War II the Eastern Gas and Fuel Company had stored gas in an even larger tank near the current site of the LNG terminal. That tank was the largest on the Eastern seaboard—about 15 stories tall. The LNG terminal in Everett seemed a trivial risk by comparison (McCarthy interview, 3/10/89).

Everett residents also expected a series of direct benefits from the LNG terminal that would outweigh health risks. Everett is a working-class community. The Exxon industrial complex has supplied jobs for local inhabitants for many years. Five of the seven aldermen of the city government even worked at the Exxon complex at the time of the LNG decision. Furthermore, tax revenues collected from companies in Everett substantially reduced real estate taxes of local residents (McCarthy, interview 3/10/89). Distrigas paid over a million dollars each year in property taxes to Everett (*Leader Herald*, 5/18/78). Few residents cared, therefore, what happened to Everett gas.

Very few people were concerned when Fay from MIT estimated that up to 20,000 residents could be fatally burned by an ignited vapor cloud. Nor were they concerned when he mentioned Everett, East Boston, and Chelsea as the prime risk locations. Instead, only a few Everett residents, some Cambridge supporters (about 20), and members of the Union of Concerned Scientists (UCS) appeared at the public hearing to oppose the FPC's decision.

These few Everett residents were part of the Massachusetts chapter of Bring Legal Action and Stop the Tanks (BLAST). They had become aware of the LNG threat following a "60 Minutes" exposé of the New York tragedy when a storage tank had caught fire. Once awakened to the threat,

MassBLAST started to campaign about the discrepancies in estimates being raised by Fay and the UCS. Although the group managed to gain some notice from city officials, it never swayed the federal judge during the Washington hearings (Fay interview, 6/9/87; McCarthy interview, 6/5/87).

The administrative law judge reviewing the FPC decision supported the agency despite the citizens' and Fay's criticism. The final ruling in Washington, D.C., approved the application of Distrigas. The company was authorized to sell imported LNG to interstate customers, and to construct and operate the LNG terminal. The judge's attitude overall was that the LNG terminal was safe and without any reasonable health risk. He agreed with the FPC's worse-case analysis, and stated that the risks were probably lower than predicted by the agency. Evidence of lower risks, he claimed, was the small probability of a shipping collision estimated by the FPC, and the Coast Guard's traffic scheme reducing the probability of a collision. In this light of lower risks, the judge questioned the validity of Fay's testimony (Fay interview, 6/9/87; Arvelund interview 6/10/87).

In sum, the LNG case in Everett, Massachusetts, was clearly a decision by the FPC that was never challenged by Everett residents. Most residents felt that direct benefits in jobs and tax revenues justified any new risks owing to terminal expansion. They also felt that Professor Fay's estimation of scientific risk was not sufficient to merit opposing the FPC or local authorities. Does this relationship between FPC bureaucrats and citizens reflect a bargaining exchange of health risk for concessions?

A Bargain Ignoring Uncertainty

Why should a unilateral decision made by a regulatory agency be treated as a bargain with citizens? A bargain is basically a mutual exchange. In economics, it occurs when a seller supplies a good and gets paid by a buyer who gains the good. The basic exchange is the good for money. In decisions on involuntary risks, the bargain is two-pronged (see Figure 1).

First, the agency sponsors a project with a local risk in order to gain benefits for the general public. For example, the local risk of an LNG terminal is the chance of fatality of nearby residents if an ignition were to occur. The concession to the public may be a new supply of imported gas for home and industrial heating.

But a second exchange may also occur, depending upon the demands of citizens who incur the risks. Industries or companies generating the risk may provide citizens with personal gains such as jobs or tax revenues

Figure 1
Bargaining on Expansion of LNG Terminal

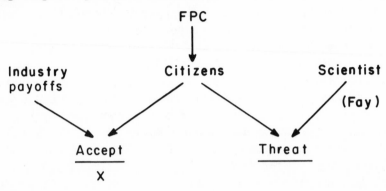

to reduce property taxes. In this way, a decision could be treated as a bargain that exchanges personal risks for personal gains or public benefits.

The bargaining problem was solved from the beginning in the LNG case. The Everett residents would suffer negligible health risks so that New England and Mid-Atlantic industries and households could gain concessions. In return, the Everett residents would gain personal concessions from local industrial firms. These concessions include jobs, tax revenues to reduce property taxes, and industrial services. Thus, both the first and second exchanges of risks for concessions already existed for Everett residents. All the FPC had to do was to preserve the faith of citizens in the expertise of the bureaucrats and their scientists, and in the power of the agency to make effective decisions.

Regarding knowledge, citizens of Everett were not even interested in Professor Fay's critical remarks about the magnitude of the population exposed to the risk. They continued to trust the FPC and its scientific consultant, SAI, which claimed that the probability of a risk ever occurring was negligible.

Why should the citizens not trust this probability of a risk occurring? Professor Fay had never questioned the probability of an LNG tanker accident, leak of LNG, vapor cloud formation, or instantaneous ignition. He probably agreed that this probability of risk was negligible. He had, however, criticized the magnitude of exposure of the population to such a risk. Not 2,500 but instead 20,000 residents could die. Fay emphasized that even though the probability of an accident was negligible, the deleterious effect in human fatalities was unacceptable.

The two key resources were knowledge and power. "Knowledge" refers here to the use of scientific information that is certain. Such knowledge of agencies is in question only if experts claim inconsistencies in the interpretation of the data used. In the LNG case, Fay claimed an inconsistency in the calculation of the magnitude of population exposure, but not of the probability of being exposed to a risk.

"Power" refers here simply to the "ability to prevail in conflict and to overcome obstacles" (Deutsch 1968: 22). Thus, in a bargaining situation, power refers to the ability of the agency and industries to pressure citizens into implementing decisions, despite scientific information that may not be certain. In the LNG case, the threat of knowledge by Fay was insufficient to jeopardize the bargain. Citizens were content to believe in the expertise and power of bureaucrats to make effective decisions.

The bargain thus remained simple in the LNG case (see Figure 1). Why were the citizens in the dioxin case, by contrast, apparently not convinced by their agency's bargain? Were the risks unacceptable, or were personal concessions lacking?

THE DIOXIN CASE

A bargain does not appear to have been struck between the agency and citizens in the dioxin case. Citizens would not take *any* health risks in exchange for personal concessions. Moreover, the critical scientist played a key role as both educator and technical spokesman for the citizens. The result was strong opposition from both the citizens and the scientist. Even the agency's effort to build consensus among scientists was to no avail. Still, neither citizens nor scientist could compel the regulatory agency to change its decision.

The primary challenge to the Department of Sanitation's proposal for a municipal waste incinerator came from residents of Brooklyn adjacent to the proposed site. These were led by the Community Boards of Community District 1 (including Greenpoint and Williamsburg), District 2 (Heights-Ft. Greene) and District 3 (Bedford-Stuyvesant). Although New York City had been discussing incinerators since the late 1960s, residents of these three districts were not affected until 1983, when the DOS started to investigate incineration as a disposal option.

In the early 1980s, most Brooklyn residents neither knew that dioxin was a by-product of incineration nor that it was a health risk if inhaled, consumed, or touched. Once they learned of its undisputed carcinogenic effects, they became strongly opposed to the siting of the new incinerator. They did not want to be "paid off" by new jobs that would become available (Romalewski interview, 3/10/89; Blackstone interview, 3/10/89).

In addition to the Community Boards, there were at least two organizations that helped lead the opposition to the incinerator. These were the Hasidic Jewish community in Williamsburg and the Coalition for a Safe Environment (CASE). Hasidic Jews are a very orthodox religious group composed primarily of immigrants from Hitler's persecution during World War II. The United Jewish Organization, (UJO), which comprises all Jewish congregations and organizations, helped to coordinate this group (Stauber interview, 3/13/89; Schnitzler interview, 6/30/87).

CASE was also an organization that focused solely on the incinerator project. Although it existed earlier, the leaders of CASE used the incinerator dispute to revitalize the organization. These leaders were primarily one resident and one critical scientist from the Center for Biological and Natural Systems, biologist Barry Commoner. The organization constituted an umbrella for several local neighborhood and block groups. Its primary members, however, were Hasidic Jews and blacks who helped in grass roots mobilizing. During the peak of the challenge to the DOS in 1984–85, CASE constituted a total of 350,000 people, comprising all of its block associations (Blackstone interview, 3/10/89).

The Hasidic community and CASE took the lead. They could benefit from the publicity and increased membership, but they also had a desire to win the battle over this new risk. They claimed that the Brooklyn Navy Yard was an inappropriate site for several reasons. Most important, residents were concerned that concentrations of dioxin and furans would be high in the ambient air surrounding their homes. This could lead to numerous cases of cancer among residents. Many children—7 to 8 per family in Hasidic families—would be particularly vulnerable to this incidence of cancer. Residents did not understand why such a facility had to be located in a densely populated neighborhood (Dereszewski interview, 6/24/87; Commoner interview, 8/12/87; Schnitzler interview 6/30/87). Nearly 10,000 residents showed up at a rally in Williamsburg to voice these views (Commoner et al. 1985: 3).

The predominant fear of residents was initiating cancer from exposures to dioxin. They did not trust the "precise" estimates of levels of risk analyzed by scientists. As one citizen put it, how could scientists be precise in their calculations when there was little certain knowledge, little experimentation, no testing of models, and only computer simulations based on gross assumptions about dioxin emission rates (Frischman interview, 3/10/89)?

Another issue was that citizens saw risk as a yes/no option, not a variable option as did scientists. One rabbi summed up the perplexing issue of variable levels of risk: "How many deaths is garbage worth?"

When asked whether reduced levels of risk would be more desirable, residents generally confirmed that no "little bit" was acceptable. Their reason was that scientists could not estimate levels precisely. Besides, different risks accumulate, and no one had looked at this problem. Residents did agree, however, that if the incinerator presented *no* risk at all, then they would be willing to see it sited nearby (interviews with Frischman, 3/10/89; Levy, 3/13/89; Cole, 3/14/89; Stauber, 3/13/89, Sikes, 3/14/89).

Residents were even more adamant about not focusing on disagreements between scientists. If residents did not believe in scientific estimates, why should they worry about disagreements over estimates? As one resident recounted, different experts have risk estimates that are convincing, yet contradictory. She decided to make an intuitive judgment of the level of dioxin risk, and then to favor the scientist who approximated her position.

Another resident said she knew about scientific disagreement because the New York Public Interest Research Group (NYPIRG) had told her. Her response to the disagreement, however, was to become more suspicious of the DOS and Board of Estimate in siting the incinerator. This suspicion of city agencies was shared generally by all residents. This was a great change from the start, when residents had not been mistrustful of the incinerator as first proposed (interviews with Frischman, 3/10/89; Levy, 3/13/89; Cole, 3/14/89; Sikes, 3/14/89).

NYPIRG strongly supported these residents who opposed the incinerator. The organization is a nonprofit, research group composed of lawyers and scientists that monitors toxic projects. The perspective on this project was that incineration is a political but not a functional solution to the crisis of leaking landfills. NYPIRG instead advocates recycling as the best solution. One of the members of NYPIRG played a key role in organizing CASE to oppose the incinerator (Romalewski interview, 3/10/89).

A second potential advocacy group was the Citizens Advisory Committee (CAC). This group consisted of the collective interests of residents, the city, and environmental groups. Membership in CAC, however, underrepresented residents. Only 3 of the 28 members were residents. Nevertheless, CAC was particularly critical of the site selection process. It also requested a delay in the public review until further tests of dioxin emissions and health effects could be completed. At that point, safe operational procedures could be outlined for the plan (Meyer interview, 6/24/87; Dereszewski interview 6/24/87; *The Phoenix*, 4/11/85). CAC's position was to exert control over the procedures of operation in order to insure public safety. Ultimately, the organization abstained from voting for or against the incinerator, because of the scientific uncertainty about the dioxin issue.

The third potential advocacy group was environmentalists. Surprisingly, however, environmental groups favored the proposal of the DOS to construct the incinerator. Different from NYPIRG, these groups believed that the incineration of waste would protect public health more than would leaking landfills in New York State. They did not focus on recycling, which had not been raised as an alternative option. Thus, the DOS gained full support of the National Resources Defense Council (NRDC), the Sierra Club, and the Environmental Defense Fund (EDF) (Commoner interview, 8/12/86).

Commoner was the only scientist who gained the trust and respect of the residents. He became both their educator and spokesperson. This was quite a contrast from the LNG case, in which residents had not cared what the scientist Fay had to say. Commoner's role started off as an educator of the citizens. He clarified how dangerous were the emissions of dioxin gases and particulates that would be released from the incinerator stack. Commoner's main role, however, was to speak scientifically on behalf of residents. Residents respected him as a scientist because they had intuitively determined that only he held a justifiable position on the siting issue. This benefited residents, but it also gave Commoner a political impact using scientific evidence.

Residents believed that Commoner was critical to the effectiveness of their opposition. He was credible, competent, and experienced in protesting environmental issues. He also represented a university, and was a "big name." Most important, he could present the scientific evidence as "facts." Residents felt that without Commoner, their opposition would have been discounted by the DOS as idealistic and uninformed (interviews with Commoner, 4/15/89; Frischman, 3/10/89; Levy, 3/13/89; Stauber, 3/13/89; Cole, 3/14/89; Sikes, 3/14/89). Other residents, however, became disappointed in Commoner for his media orientation, difficulty in communicating simply to residents, and inability to provide information to help grass roots organizing (Blackstone interview, 3/10/89).

Despite the waning interest of citizens in science, Commoner still used scientific uncertainty about the probability of risk to challenge the DOS's support for the incinerator. The key threat was the two order-of-magnitude difference between Commoner's and Hart's risk estimates, assuming different emission rates of dioxin. At Commoner's emission rate, the chance of residents initiating cancer was as high as one in a thousand for those exposed over a lifetime. Residents could claim that any agency proposing such health risks was not protecting the health and safety of citizens. Moreover, the DOS's claim that the incinerator would benefit the public interest of New York City by providing another disposal facility for the city's garbage seemed suspicious. What public benefit was worth a trade of people's lives?

But the second basis of the threat to residents was also important. Commoner argued that the experts were focusing on the *same* emissions rate assumed by Hart, the DOS, and Commoner (respectively, 6 and 29 cases of cancer per million people exposed over a lifetime). Both of these estimates were *higher* than the acceptable *de minimis* level of risk of one case of cancer per million people exposed to a pollutant over a lifetime. At either risk estimate, therefore, Commoner argued that the DOS should not site the incinerator in the Brooklyn Navy Yard (Commoner interview, 3/15/89).

In order to overcome this opposition led by Commoner, the DOS called in the New York Academy of Sciences to settle the scientific issues for the NYC Board of Estimate. The Academy brought in a group from MIT to lead a one-day facilitation session. A facilitation is the least interventionist form of mediation, which is assisted by a neutral coordinator.

On December 18, 1984, 55 men and women gathered at the Academy. Engineers, public health specialists, epidemiologists, and environmental scientists took part in the panel to address the scientific issues. The audience was members of the BOE. The facilitation occurred primarily between the panel and the BOE. Commoner and some representatives of the Brooklyn Community Districts (CDs) were allowed to ask questions afterward.

Three issues most concerned the BOE. These were the nature of the dioxin risk, whether that risk could be reduced, and the nature of health impacts of dioxin emissions (Susskind and Cruikshank 1987: 157). The main disagreement in the discussion was over the choice of risk estimate by the DOS. Gaps in basic research were noted, and competing theories of dioxin formation and destruction discussed as a function of combustion temperatures and oxygen flow. Other issues concerned the reliability of various dioxin control filters, and extrapolations from animal tests to human risks. Disputes arose over data samples, ways experts framed questions, and whether "worst-case" analysis required an extreme or only "reasonable" choice of parameter value (Susskind and Cruikshank 1987: 158–160). Toward the end of the session, all participants had a better understanding of the critical scientific issues, although these were not resolved.

According to the facilitator, Dr. Lawrence Susskind (personal communication, 3/20/89), a hypothetical consensus did emerge between Commoner and the BOE. This occurred because the facilitator shifted his question to risk management rather than continuing to focus only on risk assessment. Commoner agreed that he would support the construction of the incinerator based on three conditions: (1) a dioxin-monitoring procedure would be initiated, (2) the incinerator would be permanently closed if it ever emitted more dioxin than permitted according to the state standard (later revoked in 1985), and (3) liability for all accidents would be covered by the city or the builder (Susskind and Cruikshank 1987: 160). The BOE agreed to make such arrangements. This consensus was hypothetical, however, because neither the full BOE nor the full body of Brooklyn residents were present at the session. An effective agreement could not exist without full participation.

The consensus therefore eroded only months later by a unanimous vote of the Community Boards (CBs) from the Brooklyn districts. They voted not to approved the siting of the incinerator. The CBs of all three community districts rejected the proposed facility in a 100 percent vote in April 1985. In May, however, the City Planning Commission scheduled a public hearing on the plant, before certifying the Final Environmental Impact Statement. The Planning Commission used its unilateral authority as a regulatory body to overturn the CBs vote by approving construction in July 1985. The BOE followed by also voting 6 to 5 in favor of construction in August 1985. The construction of the incinerator was to be an outcome of the Uniform Land Use Review Process (ULURP). This final vote of the BOE authorized the DOS to enter into a contract with a selected vendor (Respondents Position Schiff et al. v. BOE et al., N.Y. Supreme Court 1985: 8).

Uncertainty as a Bargaining Resource

Both the dioxin and LNG cases show that disagreements among scientists were insufficient to change regulatory decisions. Even in close association with protesting citizens groups (dioxin case), scientific uncertainties are a threat but not a block to agency decision-making. This section interprets the findings in the dioxin case as an example of bargaining when scientific uncertainty is used as a bargaining resource.

The potential for a bargain in the dioxin case appears to have eroded from the start (see Figure 2). Citizens became critical of the proposed new incinerator. They immediately joined a scientist who confirmed their belief that the level of risk was much higher than the DOS had claimed.

Figure 2
Bargaining on Municipal Waste Incinerator in Brooklyn

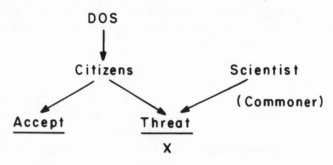

The citizens were unwilling to accept this new level. Furthermore, they refused to agree to personal concessions to make the DOS's level of risk more acceptable. In this sense, neither exchange occurred: no citizen accepted the health risk proposed by the DOS, and no citizen agreed to be paid off in personal concessions.

Why did this erosion of bargaining occur? Both the key resources of knowledge and power were threatened. Let us investigate who launched these threats and why they eroded the belief in agency expertise and decision-making.

Knowledge: In Doubt. An important step in the dioxin case was that citizens linked up with a scientist in order to criticize the DOS and its consultant. I have referred to this type of union between residents and a scientist as a "smart public" (Klapp 1988). This partnership is "smart" in that Commoner disputed risks scientifically on behalf of the residents. But the partnership was also powerful because residents demanded concessions from the agency, such as the relocation or redesign of the facility. Smart publics often involve environmentalists, citizens, or workers linked with scientists. Environmental groups in Pennsylvania, Rhode Island, New Jersey, and New Hampshire have convinced Commoner to assist their fights against the siting of toxic waste incinerators (Commoner 1984: 34). Of course, the scientific staffs of organizations such as the National Resource Defense Council and the Sierra Club have constituted smart publics for many years.

These links between citizens and scientists have not been without internal problems. In the dioxin case, for example, Brooklyn residents were suspicious of all risk estimates and "risk levels" of scientists. They did not trust the scientific methods of the experts, and did not care, therefore, whether scientists disagreed with one another. But they did care about political stances. Commoner took their same political stand against the incinerator. Citizens were willing, therefore, to have more confidence in Commoner's ability to assess the health risks at stake. Based on this smart public, Commoner saw his opportunity to use uncertainty in the scientific research to challenge the agency's estimates.

Let us examine Commoner's specific uses of risk issues and scientific uncertainties in the dioxin case (Commoner et al. 1984). Risk issues include levels (or probabilities) of risk, numbers of people exposed, natures of risk, and pathways of exposure. As analyzed in Chapter 2, uncertainties could represent data, extrapolation, models, or parameter questions.

For Commoner, the first step was to raise uncertainties about data and parameters. Here is where he effectively attacked the level of risk presented by the DOS. Commoner introduced different scientific data on dioxin emissions rates that were equally valid to those provided by the DOS and Hart. Recorded tests of extremely high dioxin emissions rates from the Hampton incinerator were equally valid to estimates of low dioxin emission rates from the Chicago incinerator used by the agency and Hart. Although equally valid, these were still scientifically inconclusive data. The aim, however, was to throw doubts on the regulatory judgment of the agency. If the DOS agreed to new data on dioxin emissions, it would effectively agree that the probability of cancer risk was much higher than initially claimed.

Commoner therefore needed to establish that the probability of dioxin exposure to local residents was much higher than projected by the DOS. The dioxin emissions rate is directly linked to the concentration of dioxin compounds in gaseous or particulate form. If Commoner could demonstrate a change of greater than one order of magnitude in emissions rate, the estimated risk of cancer would also be increased by that amount. This variable, dioxin emission rate, was therefore an essential feature of Commoner's critique.

Commoner's second step was to reduce model uncertainty. He validated his own model of risk by showing how similar it was to Hart's. Using the same dioxin emission rate, Commoner demonstrated that Hart's and his own model of predicted risk estimates were, respectively, 6 and 29 excess cases of cancer per million people exposed over a lifetime. This difference of only one order of magnitude was small enough to be scientifically insignificant, taking into account the range of statistical uncertainties in both models.

Commoner also reduced uncertainty regarding the initiation of cancer. Both he and Hart used similar cancer models. As a result, their estimates of dose-responses in the population would be similar.

Finally, Commoner emphasized the precarious nature of the DOS decision. He asserted that both Hart's and his own risk estimates, using either similar or different parameters, were *above* the agency's regulatory limit. The *de minimis* level for most regulatory agencies of the federal government is to regulate when risks are above one chance of death per million people exposed to a pollutant over a lifetime. Commoner therefore argued that from a regulatory standpoint the incinerator should not be sited in the Brooklyn Navy Yard because the range of possible risk was too high.

Commoner thus assisted residents to challenge the knowledge of the agency. His primary threat was aimed at the dioxin emissions rates, since Commoner and the DOS shared the same basic risk and cancer dose-response models. By forming a smart public, residents linked with Commoner could now question the DOS's level of risk. Uncertainties were not acceptable in the data and in the dioxin emissions parameter.

Have such smart publics maintained the quality of scientific knowledge? The production of research by scientists, I argue, *has* been relatively insulated from societal pressures as was originally thought (Mazur 1973, 1981). The dioxin case shows that Commoner did not create a dispute over cancer models, when there was little difference between his and Hart's estimates of risk due to those models. Instead, he focused the dispute only on the data and parameter uncertainties that did reflect legitimate scientific disagreements. I therefore differ with Mulkay (1979), who suggests that scientific knowledge is always politically determined. But once scientific knowledge becomes used as a political resource, I do agree that scientific norms no longer enable scientists to behave in politically neutral ways, as was originally expected (Mulkay 1979: 110). Moreover, the role of scientists in this case shows that politics does not become more impartial. Instead, Mulkay quite rightly claims that scientists such as Commoner act according to political norms in the political arena. They use their "certified" knowledge to further their own or others' interests (Mulkay 1979) and to undermine opponents such as the DOS. Once relatively impartial scientific knowledge enters the political arena, therefore, I agree that politics can determine how scientists like Commoner use that knowledge instrumentally.

Power: Threatened but Not Yet Unseated. A key condition of decision-making power is deference. "Deference" refers here to the willingness of interest groups to yield to the judgment of government bureaucracies about which health risks to authorize and which to limit (Kelman 1981). As long as citizens defer, the agency has relatively complete power to make decisions. But when citizens refuse to defer, citizens must try to negotiate a new relationship in which they "share" the power to make decisions. How much power is shared, however, depends upon how much political influence citizens can bring to bear on decisions.

The basis for increasing the power of citizens to bargain with agencies is based on at least two factors. The first is the unwillingness of citizens to defer to the agency. This we have referred to as *holding out*. Once the agency makes an offer of a decision, and the citizens refuse to accept the offer, this constitutes the first step in holding out. If offers of concessions are consistantly made by the agency, and are slowly rejected by citizens, this constitutes a period of holding out.

In the dioxin case, residents immediately rejected the proposed decision to site the incinerator. Only after delaying for some months did a group of citizens agree to a hypothetical bargain struck by Commoner during the DOS-sponsored facilitation. But most residents were not present at this negotiation, and thus continued to refuse health risks or personal concessions.

The second important factor for increasing citizen power relative to the agency depends upon the resources directly under the control of the citizens. One resource we discussed is to align with a scientist to form a "smart public," thus gaining access to a wide body of new scientific knowledge and data. Agencies, however, may argue that neither scientists nor their information carry much political weight when research is highly uncertain. In Commoner's case, his credibility as a professional scientist was challenged because he had taken an ideological position consistently defending citizen's groups.

Another resource is that influential citizens may have important ties to political, financial, or technological groups from which the agency wishes to benefit. Had Brooklyn citizens held specific personal connections with top directors at Signal, the multinational construction company entitled to build the incinerator, the DOS might have been more willing to concede to citizens' health wishes in return for their influence at Signal. Had residents had the ability to promise solid blocs of votes for elected officials, for instance, this would have created another indirect channel of influence on the DOS. Finally, had Brooklyn neighborhoods been powerful lobbies at the City Planning Commission or the BOE, they might have pressured the DOS to make concessions. But neither CASE nor the Hasidic community could overcompensate for the politics between BOE, DOS, and Signal. The lieutenant governor of New York became the head of the Signal Corporation.

The citizens therefore stood to gain or to lose by trying to extract concessions through bargaining. If citizens represented a significant base of power, then they stood to gain concessions from the agency. But if citizens did not have this base of power, then they could only hope for a few concessions from the agency. These would constitute personal payoffs to make the risk worth tolerating. But the citizens of Brooklyn did not even want these payoffs.

Whereas the citizens retained power by holding out, the DOS and BOE clearly gained power through *extended bargaining*. Brooklyn citizens were not invited to participate in the facilitation organized by the DOS and BOE. Instead, these agencies invited agency scientists and other members of the scientific and technical community. Commoner was asked to join residents as an observer, rather than as a scientist. Nevertheless, some consensus did emerge between the scientists, the BOE, and Commoner, with the apparent approval of the residents in the audience.

The use of unassisted and assisted negotiation to resolve disputes over health, safety, and environmental risks has increased substantially in recent years (see Susskind and Cruikshank 1987; Harter 1982; Fisher and Ury 1981; Raiffa 1983). These are prescriptive and instrumental forms of bargaining, not just analytic devices. The premise is that concerned or "stakeholding" groups can reach consensus through informal, face-to-face interaction in which all groups seek to achieve their objectives rather than to accept win-lose or compromise decisions. Susskind and Cruikshank (1987: 11–17, 19–20) argue that such negotiated settlements of disputes avoid both the stalemates of classical bargaining when both sides try to win. They also avoid the refusals to honor compromises because demands were too meek or concessions too unrealistic.

According to Harter (1982), several criteria determine a successful negotiation. First, negotiations must promise an outcome for parties that is as good or better than their alternatives. Second, parties must not be intractable, or concessions will be impossible. Finally, a limited number of parties (15), a deadline, and a method of implementing final agreements must be approved by the parties. Whether a negotiated agreement endures depends upon whether realistic, modest, and feasible commitments have been made. Parties tend to make unrealistic promises when they either are "lured into a spirit of harmony" or have ignored scientific, legal, or other obstacles in anticipation of an agreement (Susskind and

Cruikshank 1987: 31-32). In the dioxin case, the facilitation that occurred was not intended to reconcile residents and agencies to a better bargain. Instead, it was intended to resolve the scientific issues about which the BOE was in doubt.

The bargain was for residents to accept the health risks of the incinerator in exchange for benefits of monitoring, emergency closure, and accident liability (Susskind personal communication, 3/20/89). But residents of the Brooklyn neighborhoods did not want such a bargain. Most residents were unwilling to accept any health risks of the incinerator, despite concessions. Residents wanted an offer from the DOS or BOE to relocate the incinerator, but these citizens were not powerful enough to gain that offer.

BARGAINING THEORY

The purpose of this section is to review the conventional models of bargaining under uncertainty, and to propose my own analysis. We first discuss economic theories of sequential bargaining with incomplete information. These treat equal exchange relationships based on uncertainties about preferred decisions. We then review the models of hierarchical relationships within public organizations. These hierarchies and uncertainties are more appropriate to the agency-citizen interaction. But such models treat the citizen rather than the agency as the actor with primary control. Finally, I propose the Bureaucratic Bargain analysis. This analysis is based on hierarchy, accommodates uncertain information, and places the regulatory agency in the role of convincing citizens or industrialists to comply with its decision.

Economic Bargains: Sequential Bargaining with Incomplete Information

My treatment of bargaining draws from recent game theory on sequential bargaining with incomplete information. I refer specifically to Sutton's (1986) discussion of the Sobel-Takahashi model (1983), following the treatment of Fudenberg and Tirole (1983).

The basic game is between two players, generally one buyer and one seller trying to agree on a price for an indivisible good. This detour from relations between regulator and citizen is necessary in order to understand how uncertainty is treated in a game theoretic model. If the players had perfect information about each other's price preferences, an agreement could be struck immediately. Thus "information" refers to the decision preferences of the other player, not to the technical understanding needed to calculate a price.

Because information is not complete, however, bargaining must be iterative or "sequential." Information is incomplete only on one side: the seller lacks full information about the buyer's price preferences. But the buyer knows how much both he and the seller value the good. To discover the buyer's willingness to accept a price, the seller must continue to offer prices that are then accepted or rejected by the buyer.

Assume, by analogy, that the buyer is the citizen, and the seller, the agency bureaucrat. The good is the environmental risk, and the price is the proposed decision. A simple bargain occurs when the citizen (buyer) agrees to the first price offered by the agency bureaucrat (seller). Following each rejected offer, the bureaucrat's/seller's belief about what is an acceptable price is adjusted. The longer the period of offers and replies, the lower is the price and also the more complete is the bureaucrat's/seller's information about citizen/buyer preferences. Clearly, the incentive is for the citizen/buyer to continue to reject the bureaucrat's/seller's offers up to the point where the latter threatens to seek some other option (Sutton 1986: 717, 719).

What we need, however, is a bargaining analysis based on an involuntary and hierarchical rather than a voluntary and equal relationship between agency and citizen. The analysis should treat uncertainty in technical information as well as in preferences among existing decisions.

The Principal-Agent Model

The principal-agent model is discussed by Moe (1984) and Mitnick (1980) (earlier by Niskanen [1971]) in the new economics of bureaucracy. The model was originally developed to deal with risk taking and incomplete information in economic contexts (Ross 1973; Spence and Zeckhauser 1971).

This model is useful to us because Moe (1984) focuses specifically on the hierarchical relationships between citizen and politician. The model assumes conflict of interest and asymmetries of information between parties. Moe also examines similar relationships between politician and bureaucrat, and has alluded to that between citizen and bureaucrat. It is the latter relationship to which we now turn. According to Moe (1984: 756), the relationship is the following: "The *principal* considers entering into a contractual agreement with another, the *agent*, in the expectation that the agent will subsequently choose actions that produce outcomes desired by the principal" (emphasis added). According to Moe's model, the principal would appear to be the citizen. This principal enters a contractual agreement with the agent, here the bureaucrat of the regulatory agency. The citizen's expectation is that the bureaucrat will make decisions in the interest of citizens.

This relationship is problematic, however, because control is not divided clearly. A citizen could enter such an agreement for at least two reasons. First, the agent (the bureaucrat) might have specialized technical knowledge needed to make certain regulatory decisions. But that information may only be imperfectly accessible to the citizen (Moe 1987: 480). Second, the task of regulation might be too large and complex for the citizen to handle (Moe 1984: 756). Again, this means that performance is only imperfectly controlled by the citizen (Moe 1987: 480). Once having entered the contract with the agent/bureaucrat, the key problem for the principal/citizen is how to ensure that the agent continues to pursue the principal's interests. This is a problem because the agent/bureaucrat has his or her own interests. Thus, the principal/citizen must structure monitoring, rewards, and sanctions to make it advantageous for the agent/bureaucrat to serve the principal's interests (Moe 1984: 756–757). In the worst case, however, the citizen must expect "slippage" between the desired and the achieved performance of the bureaucrat (Moe 1987: 481).

Similar to the game-theoretic bargaining model, "uncertainty" can be interpreted as the imperfect information of the decision that the agent/bureaucrat prefers. But the principal-agent model goes a step further than the gaming model. It also attributes "uncertainty" to the imperfect technical information that the agent uses to choose that imperfect decision (Moe 1984: 756, 766). This latter reference, we infer, might be about scientific information.

"Opposition," instead, must be inferred indirectly. The agent/bureaucrat can behave in ways that produce outcomes contrary to the interests of the principal/citizen. The more often this occurs, the more frequently the principal/citizen will try to oppose the agent. This form of "opposition," however, can only be analyzed in terms of the structure of incentives and monitoring that the citizen uses to keep the agent "on track."

The strengths of this model for our purposes are clearly the hierarchical treatment of the citizen-bureaucrat relationship and the treatment of uncertainty in terms of the performance of the bureaucrat. Thus, uncertainty represents imperfect information about the preferred decisions of the agent/bureaucrat, and the inputs such as scientific understanding upon which those preferences are based.

But the model does not satisfactorily simulate the citizen-bureaucrat relationship as evidenced in the dioxin case, for example. In this case, the hierarchical relationship is one in which the DOS depends upon whether residents agree to the decisions proposed by the agency. That is, can the DOS—not the residents—get what it wants. The agency, therefore, is really in the role of "principal," while the citizen is in the role of the "agent."

Moe agrees that the relationship between the bureaucrat and citizen is problematic for the principal-agent model. The bureaucrat starts off as the citizen's agent, but the authority role shifts to the bureaucrat who gains control (Moe, personal communication, 2/1/88). Let us reverse this hierarchical relationship, then, and integrate it into a Bureaucratic Bargaining framework.

The Bureaucratic Bargain

In my analysis, the bureaucrat and citizen are in a hierarchical relationship (Klapp 1989). The bureaucrat is in a dominant decision-making position relative to the citizen. Yet the bureaucrat has an incentive to make some concessions, in order to gain citizen cooperation.

In proposing the LNG terminal expansion and the construction of the municipal waste incinerator, both regulatory agencies wanted citizens to agree to nominally small risks of fatality. The Everett citizens agreed immediately to a bargain, but Brooklyn citizens demanded instead that the risk be eliminated (or relocated) to make a bargain worthwhile.

The bureaucrat represents the executive branch of government. He or she has the legal right through legislative mandate to make decisions about where to site facilities and at what level to set standards of exposure to carcinogens. Bureaucrats in both the FPC and DOS could use their official discretion to implement respective construction and siting decisions regardless of citizen response.

But these bureaucrats also want to gain two benefits. The first is the voluntary compliance of the citizen in approving and implementing a decision. He or she does not want to go to court in order to force compliance. Bureaucrats at the DOS wanted the residents of Brooklyn to agree voluntarily to the incinerator siting, just as Everett residents had complied with expansion of the LNG terminal.

The second gain for the bureaucrat is to "look good" in administering regulatory decisions. The FPC appeared very effective in gaining compliance from most residents of Everett. The DOS, by contrast, had little choice but to withstand the resistance and potential threats of Brooklyn residents.

These potential gains provide the incentive for the bureaucrat to negotiate with citizens for decisions that are mutually satisfactory. The expectation of the bureaucrat is that citizens will eventually agree to a proposed decision as initially offered (or a minor variant).

But these gains require that the bureaucrat make some concessions to the citizen. The bureaucrat may have to refrain from making unilateral decisions, therefore, and instead cooperate with citizens in order to achieve voluntary compliance. The expansion of the LNG terminal posed no problems, since most citizens agreed to it from the start, and demanded nothing from the agency in return. They already had personal concessions of jobs and tax reductions from the industrial companies involved. But in Brooklyn, residents insisted that the DOS cooperate by *not* building the waste incinerator.

Another concession is operational. When citizens are ready to agree to a project, they often make demands regarding safeguards on operations, redesign of some technologies, or monitoring procedures. In Everett, citizens never bothered to make such specific requests. In Brooklyn, only the Citizens Advisory Committee, including city officials along with citizens, ever reached such a discussion of operational features.

In order to gain these as concessions from the bureaucrat, the citizen must also make concessions. Citizens must be willing to accept some exposure to risk. They must also take the time and effort to participate in decision-making to assure that "safe and sure" choices are being made. Although only a few citizens participated in Everett, both wealthy Brooklyn Heights and poor Brooklyn residents were avidly involved in the incinerator dispute.

The Bureaucratic Bargain is thus a hierarchical bargain between agency and citizen, with the agency dominant. Scientists and industrialists may be key participants in this debate. The agency bureaucrat wants citizens to accept the health risks voluntarily, and to help the agency "look good" administratively. In exchange, the bureaucrat is willing to make concessions to citizens. These concessions are to refrain from making unilateral decisions, and to concede safeguards, special compensation, and monitoring to make operation of the project satisfactory. Citizens should accept some exposure to risk in order to participate in cooperative decision-making. Such a risk could be less than 10^{-6} per person over a lifetime.

This approach attempts to refine and extend the analytic perspective of Nelkin (1979; Nelkin and Pollack 1981) and Sapolsky (1986). Like them, I have assumed that citizens engage experts to help fight battles over evidence that is uncertain. Citizens seek to gain a scientific voice, although they remain ambivalent about whether science is ever neutral and independent. Scientists often want the chance to apply their research, even though their expertise may be jeopardized when scientific knowledge is in question.

A bargaining approach helps specify exactly how scientific uncertainty can be used strategically by citizens. Uncertainties in the evidence and theory reveal the potential incompetence of agency bureaucrats to make decisions. This is true no matter which bureaucrat or expert analyzes the evidence. Citizens must therefore work with scientists to raise uncertainties that gain concessions on decision proposals. Bargaining with uncertainty thus offers an approach to meld experts, citizens, and bureaucrats into relationships of threats offset by concessions.

Unfortunately, bargaining efforts of citizens do not always produce bargains that are satisfactory to them. What happens when citizens in the dioxin case, for instance, resort to a more powerful option? What role does scientific information play in this new arena of intragovernmental struggle?

Chapter Four

Superseding the Bureaucracy

Regulatory decisions can be reversed when citizens gain the support of legislatures or courts. Congress can legislate to forbid agency regulations; courts can use injunctions to impede agency regulations. This chapter will provide an explanation for decision change based on both the role of uncertain scientific evidence and the delegation of authority within the U.S. government. Let us start off with some examples.

The U.S. Congress has examined regulatory proposals of agencies that obstruct the wishes of the public or industry, as in the saccharin case. In the case of ethylene dibromide (EDB), for instance, the Subcommittee on Labor Relations of the House of Representatives questioned why the Occupational Safety and Health Administration (OSHA) reluctantly enforced a safety standard for exposure to that pesticide. The hearing introduced additional information and cast doubt on the analysis done by OSHA (Krimsky and Plough 1988). But in another case on the Clinch River Breeder Reactor (CRBR), congressional politics over diverse perspectives were so divided that after 13 years of dispute, the future of the project was still unresolved (Katz 1984: 52–54).

The courts have also reprimanded agencies directly. In both the urea-formaldehyde foam insulation and benzene decisions, the Fifth Circuit Court of Appeals overturned the proposed regulations of the Consumer Product Safety Commission (CPSC) and the Occupational Safety and Health Administration. In the formaldehyde decision, the court determined that monitoring and extrapolation from rat data to human risk did not provide "substantial evidence" (Jasanoff 1986: 45).

In the benzene case, the court even decided that "significant risk" would now replace "zero-risk" as the basis for regulation to protect workers (Graham et al. 1989: 100–101).

But the court has also reinforced the decisions of some agencies, as in the final decision on dioxin. In another example, the Second Circuit Court of New York upheld OSHA on its vinyl chloride regulation. The court stated that even though the evidence was at the frontier of science, the agency had a duty to defend the health of workers (Badaracco 1985).

Such cases show that the courts and the legislature can play pivotal roles in approving or threatening regulations. In this pivotal role the bargaining resources of legislators and judges are actually bargaining rationales rather than resources. To understand this shift from "resource" to "rationale" we must review the hierarchical nature of the Bureaucratic Bargain. In the bargaining between the agency and citizens, the agency is dominant. But in the bargaining that emerges between agency or citizens and legislator or judge, the presence of a statute implies that the legislator can change the law and the judge can review the decision. This means that the agency has to give up its position of dominance in bargaining and become subordinate to the legislature or the court. The result is that the unilateral authority to act is in the hands of the legislature or the court, not the agency.

The legislature or court is not like the citizen or industrialist who needs the added support from scientific information. Instead, the legislator or judge requires only a rationale to behave as each would otherwise act. They use scientific information to legitimize their actions, not to bolster their power. It is not essential to take action, but it helps justify the decision on the basis of scientific research. Nevertheless, using such a rationale has two purposes: (1) to undermine the decision of the agency or (2) to eliminate uncertainty in order to favor the agency. The difference is that if the agency does not respond to this threat or concession by the superior actor, then that same legislator can act unilaterally to create a new decision, or the same judge can prevent the decision from being implemented. In this way, the use of science is shifted from a resource that bolsters power to a rationale that legitimizes action.

The fundamental scientific characteristic of such bargaining rationales is that evidence is usually uncertain. Defending its proposed ban of urea-formaldehyde foam insulation, the CPSC claimed that both the carcinogenicity in rats at doses comparable to human exposure and the nonrespiratory evidence of cancer in epidemiological studies showed the need for regulation. The formaldehyde industry, however, used the same data on epidemiological studies to show that the upper limit of risk was too low to justify regulation. They found no evidence of nasal cancer in humans. The scientific controversy was sufficiently keen that the Court of Appeals for the Fifth Circuit ruled that the CPSC had proposed its ban without "substantial evidence" (Gulf South Insulation v. Consumer Product Safety Commission 1983). Soon after, the EPA itself tried to stop its own spiraling scientific controversy. But eight technical panels could not resolve the underlying scientific disagreements (Jasanoff 1986: 45–52). Such cases demonstrate that scientific issues without resolution may be at the heart of many regulatory impasses.

Bargaining rationales also have political characteristics. Congress plays an assertive role in directing and critiquing agency decisions (Brickman et al. 1985). Owing to the separation of powers, the legislature sometimes unintentionally undercuts regulators. Regulatory statutes that are unchecked in their ambitiousness often neglect problems of implementation and leave agencies vulnerable to oversight. By writing statutes that lack detail, legislators require procedural checks, hearings, and reports to keep agencies in line (Brickman et al. 1985: 72–73). This preserves legislative power over agencies, and it prevents "capture" by lobbying interest groups. But oversight is also the means by which Congress critically reviews an agency's entire record of implementation. Although it legitimizes decisions because elected officials guide agencies, it also erodes public confidence by showing that agencies are incompetent on their own (Brickman et al. 1985: 95–96).

The courts are no less assertive. Through review of agency decisions, judges examine the substantive and formal procedural basis for bureaucratic choices. Laws expand judicial control over agencies by granting rights to plaintiffs to sue regulators. While the standard of judicial review is supposed to be deferential, many judgments appear to be quite aggressive. Judges can dismiss decisions that are "arbitrary, capricious, an abuse of discretion, or otherwise not in accordance with law" (Brickman et al. 1985: 114). Much scientific evidence is less precise than the "facts" judges seek. The courts therefore require extensive reports of the technical issues that engage them in inquiries that are far from deferential (Brickman et al. 1985: 114–115, 126–127).

Citizens who get a legislature or court to review a regulatory impasse achieve what is called an "outside option" in bargaining (Sutton 1986). This chapter starts off by defining such an option. It then investigates the strategies that legislators and judges use to challenge decisions. These strategies are further clarified using the notion of "burden of proof" (Brooks 1984). I apply this to the saccharin and dioxin cases, which look at the Subcommittee hearings of both the Senate and the House of

Representative, and then at court decisions of the lower Supreme Court and the Appellate Division, both of New York State. The final section of the chapter introduces my overall hypothesis about the role of scientific uncertainty in facilitating decision change.

THE "OUTSIDE OPTION"

Congress has granted citizens the right to act as watchdogs over the actions of regulatory agencies. In this way, Congress engages in what Matthew McCubbins and Thomas Schwartz (1984) call "fire alarm" rather the "police patrol" oversight of regulatory agencies. This means that member of Congress no longer need to rely on their own reviews of agencies for purposes of detecting violators. Instead, citizens utilize their own right of access to information to decry delinquent behavior to Congress. This right is established in the Freedom of Information Act. Citizens can also use public hearing, required of agencies in sections 4–7 of the Toxic Substances Control Act of 1976, to comment on agency decision-making. Finally, citizens can use their right to challenge agency decisions before courts in order to force reversals of decisions. This is facilitated by the Administrative Procedures Act of 1946 and the Environmental Procedures Act of 1969, which both give citizens legal standing against agencies. Thus, citizens have access to information, can complain about administrative decisions, and can gain remedies from the legislature and the courts (McCubbins and Schwartz 1984: 166, 174).

Fire-alarm oversight by Congress works for several reasons. Citizens have a new source of control: lobbyists can demand the attention of congressional subcommittees when legislative goals are vague. Or citizen groups can call for attention when companies violate legislative goals (McCubbins and Schwartz 1984: 172–173).

But members of Congress are also satisfied with the system. They spend less time and get more credit for agency reviews when they just focus on the violators that citizens have pointed out. And much of the cost is borne by the citizens, interest groups, regulatory agencies, or courts rather than by Congress itself (McCubbins and Schwartz 1984: 168).

Because of this system, the most frequent option is for citizens to rely first on the court and thereafter on the legislature to supersede the authority of a regulatory agency. Citizens can easily request a court injunction against an agency proposal. They do not have to demonstrate affiliation in an important constituency, and Congress has also eliminated the need of petitioners to prove personal injury in order to have "standing" to sue. Still, courts are much slower and more expensive than legislatures (Brooks, personal comment, 7/11/89). Nevertheless, citizens are harder pressed to lobby for the legislature to pass a law suspending regulatory action than simply to get the court to sue for them.

In the dioxin case, citizens successfully challenged the quality of the DOS's Environmental Impact Statement in the Supreme Court of New York. They failed to convince the higher Appellate Court, however, to place an injunction on the proposed construction of the incinerator. In the saccharin case, citizens got results from the Congress. The diet-drink industry organized diabetics, dieters, and other consumers. Together these groups lobbied Congress to pass a moratorium against the proposed FDA ban on saccharin. Both cases demonstrate that citizens can use the superseding authority of the court or legislature to reprimand regulatory agencies. Such actions are examples of "outside options" used by citizens to avoid bargaining with agencies.

In economic bargaining theory, a party uses its "outside option" when it forgos any bargain possible with another party and instead pursues some alternative course of action (Sutton 1986: 712). The option is to exit from bargaining. Roger Fisher and William Ury have also referred to the tactical importance of this option in practical interparty negotiation: a Best Alternative to a Negotiated Agreement (BATNA). They point out that no party can bargain effectively unless it knows the characteristics of its best alternative option to bargaining. Otherwise the party may accept a bargain that is too unfavorable relative to its alternatives (Fisher and Ury 1981: 104).

I accept this notion of an outside option and include it as a last resort in bargaining. Thus, an outside option is an action with superior authority that can be introduced at the last moment in a bargain to assist the weaker party. The weaker party tends to wait until evidence shows that the party cannot bargain to a desired decision on its own. This treatment of the outside option as a bargaining option changes the game significantly.

For an outside option to occur, a third party with an ability to secure an alternative agreement must be available to at least one of the two parties trying to bargain. At the same time, those two parties must disagree about the characteristics of a mutually acceptable bargain.

In my bargaining analysis, the threat of one party actually introducing the outside option is critical. Since neither party knows much about the preferences of the other regarding an acceptable bargain, neither party knows whether or when the other party will introduce the outside option. If the outside option decides in favor of the party that introduced it, the balance of power shifts. Moreover, the payoff to that party exercising the outside option is higher than if the same party was compelled to bargain until a mutually acceptable deal was struck. But if the outside option does not favor that party, then the other side does better than expected.

What is interesting about the two case studies is that outside options are more than just replacements for unsatisfactory bargains. They also offer citizens the chance to depose the authority of the regulatory agency by relying on the superior authority of the legislature or court. Moreover, the information used to depose agency authority is scientific uncertainty.

STRATEGIES FOR CHALLENGING SCIENTIFIC FINDINGS

Legislators and judges use different strategies to undercut or bolster any agency decision. If the legislator or judge wishes to bolster that decision, he can simply eliminate any discussion of scientific uncertainty. This situation was demonstrated, as we shall see, by the judge in the Appellate Division of the dioxin case. In such situations, the legislator or judge can use a political or legal strategy and neglect science entirely.

But if the legislator or judge disagrees with the agency's decision to accept or reject a risk, then scientific uncertainties can be used to undermine that decision. We will discuss the saccharin case in which legislators of Congress disagreed with the FDA's decision to ban the artificial sweetener. Legislators attempted to use scientific information to focus on uncertainty and, thus, to make the ban appear too conservative for such an uncertain risk level. We will also examine the determination of the judge in the lower New York Supreme Court that the DOS's decision to accept risks of ambient exposure to dioxin compounds was inadequate. The judge used scientific uncertainties in order to indicate a higher health risk to exposed citizens. The higher Appellate Division, however, reversed the court's final decision. It declared that there was no need to focus more on the scientific uncertainty of the case.

The legislator holds a position of power over the agency and is entitled to create the scientific strategy necessary to challenge or bolster a risk decision. This entitlement derives from the legislator's ability to persuade other legislators to reverse or modify existing legislation. This occurred, for instance, in the successive amendments to the Clean Air Act regarding auto emissions standards. The judge also holds a position of power over the agency. This position is defined in the agency's statute as one of exclusive judicial review of a decision. The judge can change or maintain the decision by choosing among scientific strategies offered by lawyers representing both sides in the dispute. In the dioxin case much of the discussion relies on strategies presented by lawyers and confirmed by judges.

A final element explains the ranking of the scientific strategies. In building theory, a scientist may work inductively from observations of data through analysis to hypotheses and theoretical explanations. But the power of scientific challenge is in reverse order. Challenges to the whole model are the most potent and move down to criticism of the sufficiency of the data base.

Following is a list of strategies that legislators or judges (lawyers) can use to threaten risk levels. Each strategy exploits some uncertainty in the scientific research. The first four strategies correlate with my four types of scientific uncertainty: model, parameter, extrapolation, and data. The latter two are new strategies that focus on whether the explanation and "regulation" are sufficient; they clearly link the analysis of uncertainty in science with the weighing of personal, social, and political values.

1. *Disputed Model*: Legislators or judges may relay on the disputes between scientists over which parameters belong in the risk model. Although this appears not to have been criticized in either the saccharin or dioxin hearings, it was raised by scientists in the LNG case. Although never challenged in the legislature or court, this uncertainty concerned whether wind speed or atmospheric turbulence would simulate the movement of a liquefied gas vapor cloud.

2. *Disputed Parameter Values*: If the model is adequate, another uncertainty that legislators or judges can challenge is how different scientists estimate parameter values. The typical controversy is over the selection of a worst case, best case, or conservative case. Even within the choice of a worst case, disputes occur over whether the most extreme value ever recorded or only a "reasonable" value should be selected. In the dioxin case, the judge in the lower Supreme Court agreed with the scientist Commoner that an insufficient worst-case dioxin emission rate had been selected by the agency, based just on the Chicago-Northwest incinerator. This incinerator actually recorded the lowest dioxin emission rate among a larger sample of incinerators.

3. *Doubtful Extrapolation*: But even if the model and parameter values are all sufficient, the legislator or judge can always insist that the extrapolation from rat tests to human risk is inadequate. In the saccharin case, all scientists at the Office of Technology Assessment and the National Academy of Sciences had determined that extrapolation was qualitatively legitimate. But they disagreed whether the methodology of extrapolation was sufficiently developed to assess quantitative risks in

humans. In particular, the notion of extrapolating from a weak animal carcinogen was doubted in the hearing of the Senate subcommittee.

4. *Insufficient Data*: Here I refer to two types, including a disputed research protocol and an inadequacy of data to make a scientific claim.

    a. *Disputed Research Protocol*: If scientific research looks good in its model, parameters, and extrapolation, the legislator or judge can still challenge the poor performance of the scientists in collecting data. This challenge can be quite devastating because it implies that the whole research may be wrong just because the underlying "facts" are wrong. In the saccharin case, the legislator in the hearing by the House Subcommittee tried to prove that the Canadian study of epidemiology was deficient in its collection of data. The FDA head, however, defied this effort to downgrade his research base.

    b. *Inadequate Data Base*: Even if the data have been collected properly, the legislator or judge can still claim that the data in the research are insufficient. Either the number of cases in the data sample is too small, or the cases have improper characteristics. Here, an excellent example occurred in the dioxin case. The judge in the lower Supreme Court insisted that a data sample of only one incinerator was too small. The agency needed to broaden its sample, particularly because the relationship between incinerator designs and emission rates was so uncertain.

5. *Disputed Explanation*: But what if the model, parameters, extrapolation method, and data are all sufficient? The legislator or judge can always challenge the explanation for risk. The saccharin case provides an interesting example. The legislator in the Senate hearing shifted the discussion of saccharin to, instead, a discussion of the impurities associated with saccharin. Although the question of impurities has no logical relevance for the carcinogenicity of saccharin (unless they can be scientifically eliminated), this issue was a powerful political factor in the debate. An entirely hypothetical argument was created about how impurities (not of saccharin) could be found to be the true carcinogens.

6. *Challenged Regulation of Uncertainty*: The last resort is for a legislator or judge to criticize whether the risk identified should be regulated. Here the risk level at which regulatory intervention should occur is not well-defined. EPA and the Consumer Product Safety Commission tend to use one chance of fatality in a million exposed persons as the *de minimis* limit. OSHA and the Nuclear Regulatory Commission (NRC) have instead used one fatality in a thousand exposed as the regulatory limit below which they need not regulate. The lack of

corresponding levels of regulated risk across agencies creates an uncertainty in itself.

BURDEN OF PROOF

Harvey Brooks (1984) claims that Congress introduced the idea of "burden of proof" in order to shift the appraisal of uncertain technical evidence to the more political question of *who* must produce more evidence. This is a question of reallocation of authority, not of searching for truth. Borrowed from legal theory, the burden of proof is based either on the existing evidence of harm to health or on the existing safety resulting from a lack of harm. The choice of definition depends upon who is being held responsible. In the saccharin case, the Delaney Clause of the statute places the burden of proof on the manufacturer to prove that a particular saccharin compound is safe. By contrast, in the dioxin case, the state Environmental Quality Review Act statute is vague, leaving the discretion to the agency to assign burden of proof. During the prodevelopment period of the 1980s, the burden of proof was implicitly assigned to opponents rather than to polluters.

Burden of proof can be conceived, I argue, according to two concepts: responsibility and standard. Responsibility indicates *who* must prove the harm or safety of the substance. In Delaney, the manufacturer was required to prove safety of saccharin; in SEQRA, the agency required the citizens to prove carcinogenicity of dioxin. The second concept, standard, indicates *what* and *how much* qualitative and quantitative evidence must be delivered to prove harm or safety. "Evidentiary rules of admissibility" and "rules of sufficiency" are the means, according to Professor Charles Nesson, by which courts determine whether juries can consider the evidence presented (Nesson 1986: 523; Wexler and Effron, 1984: 468–473).

Existing measures of the burden of proof proliferate. One is a "preponderance of evidence," in which at least 51 percent of the qualitative and quantitative "gestalt" of evidence points to one party. Another, "beyond a reasonable doubt," is used to condemn a criminal in pollution matters. The Administrative Procedures Act allows agencies to take control, using as much discretion to place burdens of proof based on even weaker evidence.

Judges generally require that regulatory agencies provide evidence according to the Administrative Procedures Act of 1946. According to this act, judges prevent agencies from proposing "arbitrary or capricious" regulations by prohibiting insufficient evidence or inadequate argument. For instance, in 1983 the Supreme Court remanded the benzene standard proposed by OSHA because the agency neglected to show by how much the risk to workers would be reduced if the exposure level was lowered tenfold (Brooks 1984: 41)

Brooks has suggested that strict guidelines be used both in restricting new substances and proposing new regulations. New substances should be "harmful until proven harmless by an overwhelming preponderance of evidence" and new standards should "not be introduced until evidence of harm from an existing standard . . . has been established with a high degree of confidence" (Brooks 1984: 41).

The APA also charges the agency with the task of making a scientific decision. The burden of proof for safety or carcinogenicity is assigned where it deems fit, subject to the constraints of its mandate. The burden is placed either on the polluter or manufacturer to prove safety, or on the citizen to prove carcinogenicity. Mandates can vary considerably in their degree of constraint: the Delaney Clause leaves the FDA with no choice about where to assign the burden of proof, whereas SEQRA leaves the Brooklyn Board of Estimate and the DOS with considerably more freedom.

A "shift" can occur in the burden of proof if either the law changes or the interpretation of the law changes. The saccharin case involved a change of law; the dioxin case involved a shift in the interpretation of a statute (responsibility switched from polluters over to citizens). Regulators who want government intervention prefer a lower standard of proof of carcinogenicity to protect the environment. Those regulators who instead want little government intervention insist on a high standard of proof of carcinogenicity.

When we look at the two case analyses of saccharin and dioxin, they fit nicely into this burden-of-proof framework. In saccharin, Congress changed the law to make potential opponents rather than the manufacturers responsible. Congress then assured that the standard of proof would be higher by insisting that impurities could not be separated from saccharin. In dioxin, by contrast, the lower court reduced the standard so that citizens could create a proof of carcinogenicity against the manufacturers of the plant. But the higher court took a more conservative perspective. It reaffirmed the agency's high standard of proof for citizens, and found that these citizens had not created an adequate proof of carcinogenicity. Let us investigate these issues of proof when citizens pursued outside options in the saccharin and dioxin cases.

DECISIONS OF THE LEGISLATURE AND COURT

The saccharin and dioxin cases show that citizens who were discontent from bargaining with agencies resorted to outside options. The saccharin case is based on hearings both of the Subcommittee on Health and Scientific Research of the U.S. Senate and the Subcommittee on Health and the Environment of the House of Representatives. Senators and representatives assessed whether scientific uncertainty about the level of saccharin risk to humans was sufficient to change the FDA's proposed ban instead to a market "labeling" decision. Congress voted and passed this as a change of law.

This shifted the responsibility of proof. Instead of saccharin being required to prove the lack of carcinogenicity, potential opponents of saccharin now had to get individual products prohibited under the guidance of Congress. I focus on the hearings in order to specify the role intended for uncertainty. Legislators often know their political position ahead of time, and can therefore choose the appropriate scientists and questions to get the interpretation they want from a hearing.

The dioxin case focuses instead on the role of the courts in offering citizens an outside option to the agency's decision. Nine residents representing primarily the Hasidic Jews in Williamsburg made a claim against the DOS. The case constitutes claims by petitioners and respondents in both the lower Supreme Court of Kings County and the higher Appellate Division regarding the Brooklyn incinerator. Initially, the lower Supreme Court decided that disagreement among scientists on dioxin emissions was sufficient reason to hold a trial with expert testimony. But the higher Appellate Division refused to assess the scientific dispute, and reversed the order for a trial. This higher court thus reinforced the agency's siting decision, even though the lower court had sided with the citizens against the incinerator.

By contrast to the shift in the responsibility of proof in the saccharin case, this dioxin case shows an adjustment of the standard of proof. The lower court assumed that the uncertainty in the scientific evidence about the level of dioxin risk was sufficient to require a new inquiry, thereby lowering the standard of proof. It ordered a trial for more scientific information. But the higher court said that more information was unnecessary, thereby reaffirming the high standard of proof set by the agency.

The Saccharin Case

In March 1977 the FDA proposed to ban saccharin. Spurred on by the diet-drink industry, the American Diabetes Association and the Juvenile Diabetes Association launched a letter-writing campaign to the FDA and to individual members of Congress. They were encouraged by the diet-drink industry, which needed either a substitute for saccharin or an approved appeal by diabetics and dieters. These citizens and industrialists attacked the FDA for proposing a ban with so uncertain and yet devastating an effect on the lives of diabetics. Saccharin might be unrelated to cancer, yet diabetics would be forced to consume sugar. Commiserating with their distress, many women dieters also wrote letters to the FDA and to their congressperson. In total, the FDA and Congress received more than 100,000 letters in six months.

The legislature twice demonstrated its power to override the FDA. These demonstrations took place in the 1977 hearings of the Subcommittee on Health and Scientific Research of the Committee on Human Resources of the U.S. Senate, and the Subcommittee on Health and the Environment of the Committee on Interstate and Foreign Commerce of the House of Representatives.

The Office of Technology Assessment of Congress had assembled a panel of recognized public health experts. The panel was asked to evaluate the scientific arguments for and against extrapolations of human saccharin risk from animal data. The OTA panel's study of *Cancer Testing Technology and Saccharin* (1977) came to conclusions that supported the positions of both the FDA and the National Academy of Sciences. Reinforcing the FDA's view, the panel concluded that "laboratory evidence demonstrates that saccharin is a carcinogen. . . . This evidence leads to the conclusion that saccharin is a potential cause of cancer in humans" (Subcommittee on Health and Scientific Research 1977: 55). But in support of NAS skepticism, the panel also found that "there are no reliable quantitative estimates of the risk of saccharin to humans" (Ibid.). Both OTA statements are scientifically valid and are mutually consistent. Although scientific findings in rats demonstrate carcinogenicity, extrapolation to humans is insufficiently understood to be trustworthy for quantitative estimates of human risk.

By June 7, 1977, Senator Edward Kennedy of Massachusetts scheduled the first Subcommittee on Health and Scientific Research (1977) hearing to examine the scientific evidence supporting the proposed ban. Present at the hearing were six committee members and six scientists from the special panel that the OTA had asked to examine the carcinogenicity of the chemical. The key commentators were Kennedy and Richard Schweiker from Pennsylvania, and the key scientists were Dr. Frederick Robbins, Dean of the Medical School at Case Western Reserve University, and. Joyce McCann, Ph.D., Senior Fellow, American Cancer Society, in residence at the University of California at Berkeley.

In his introduction to the hearing, Senator Kennedy cast doubt on the scientific rationale used by the FDA to justify the ban. He outlined two key questions: (1) Were animal carcinogens cancer-producing in humans as well? and (2) Should the government choose for the public when a risk is relatively unknown? Unclear science and arbitrary public choice were his main points. Kennedy noted that the FDA was required according to the Delaney Amendment of the Food, Drug and Cosmetics Act to place "unreasonably absolute" bans on toxic food additives despite scientific evidence that was unclear (Ibid: 1–3).

The following paragraphs investigate in detail the way that members of the Subcommittee built doubt from uncertain scientific statements. They eroded both the FDA's claim that saccharin was a human carcinogen and its policy decision that an "over-the-counter" ban without prescriptions was necessary. Both exchanges are taken from the record of the Senate hearing on June 7, 1977.

In the first exchange (which follows), Senator Kennedy started off by implicitly agreeing with the FDA. He stated that the scientists of the OTA panel were completely agreed that saccharin was a carcinogen. By the end of the interchange, however, Kennedy concluded with quite a different summary. He pointed out that it was only a "presumption" that saccharin was in fact a carcinogen in humans. This challenged the FDA's determination that animal evidence was sufficient to judge human risk.

Analysis of Senate Hearing (key phrases italicized by author for emphasis.)

Kennedy: establishes "overall agreement" among OTA panel scientists on: (1) *saccharin as a carcinogen*, (2) animal carcinogen, and (3) weak carcinogen (p. 13).

Schweiker: introduces *doubt* about whether saccharin or associated impurities are carcinogens (pp. 13–16).

Dr. Robbins (scientist), but then mostly *Dr. McCann* (scientist): responds with *nonjudgmental report of research findings* (pp. 14–16).

Schweiker: repeats the judgment that may not be *"valid"* to say saccharin is a carcinogen (p. 14).

Dr. McCann: reports more on Ames short-term testing, and how *cannot yet be "clear"* about research findings because *tests still being done* (p. 15).

Schweiker: emphasizes that tests not done means that positive *results could say* (*"pretty definitely point"*) to impurities rather than saccharin as the carcinogen (p. 15).

Dr. McCann: indicates doubt about impurities, outlines wide range of potencies possible, but agrees *could be true* (p. 15).

Kennedy: questions whether epidemiological evidence could determine the potency (p. 15).

Dr. Robbins: doubts whether it is the impurities, since would have already been evident, but agrees *we are not "absolutely sure"* (p. 15).

Kennedy: tries to *"focus at least some of the discussion"*: "I think the panel agrees that this [saccharin] is carcinogenic in terms of animals, and that it is basically a *presumption, and only a presumption*, that therefore it is carcinogenic in terms of human beings." (p. 16).

In this exchange, scientists repeated consistently that they were not certain how to interpret the scientific findings. Taking advantage of this uncertainty, Senator Schweiker questioned whether the carcinogen was actually saccharin or instead its impurities. He continued to use terms such as "valid" in order to pressure the scientists into admitting that saccharin might not be the carcinogen at all.

In the second interchange, the focus of interrogation was on a regulatory decision than had *not* been chosen by the FDA. This decision was whether to label saccharin products and keep them available in the open market. The particular constellation of interests supporting this decision was the diabetics, dieters, and, most important, the powerful diet-drink industry headed by Coca-Cola (Sapolsky 1986).

Senator Kennedy posed the question of labeling at the start of the exchange. The scientists communicated uncertainty about extrapolations from animal data to human risk and the sparse findings on human epidemiology. These scientists could not precisely determine the nature of the risk (doses, synergies), tolerable levels of risk, effects on pregnant women, or benefits to the public generally.

By the end of the interchange, scientists were asked to vote on whether the policy should be an over-the-counter ban or, instead, a freely marketed good with a label. The vote focused on the following information about tests for carcinogenicity: (1) molecular structure: carcinogen, (2) short-term test: carcinogen, (3) animal studies: in dispute, and (4) epidemiological studies: insufficient data (Subcommittee on Health and Scientific Research 1977). Three scientists voted for the ban; three other scientists voted for labels. This outcome was an implicit success for the Subcommittee, which wanted the market decision. The tie vote by scientists signaled to the Senate that it could freely pass legislation to institute labels on products in the market.

The second demonstration of power by the legislature over the FDA took place in the Subcommittee on Health and the Environment (1977) of the Committee on Interstate and Foreign Commerce of the House of Representatives in 1977. The hearing of this Subcommittee eroded conclusions that a new Canadian study (CNHWM 1977) of the epidemiology of saccharin justified the proposed FDA ban. The new Canadian study showed a significant correlation between the use of saccharin and the occurrence of bladder cancer in human males. A coincident American study, however, had shown no such correlation, but was also based on a much smaller sample.

This second hearing of the Subcommittee of the House of Representatives was chaired by Representative Paul Rogers of Florida on June 27, 1977, shortly after the Senate hearing. Present at the hearing were members of the Subcommittee including Representatives David Satterfield of Virginia, Henry Waxman of California, Andrew Maguire of New Jersey, Edward Markey of Massachusetts, and others. The key witnesses were Dr. Donald Kennedy, Commissioner, Food and Drug Administration, Department of Health, Education and Welfare; Dr. David Hamburg, President of the Institute of Medicine of the National Academy of Sciences; and Dr. Guy Newell, Acting Director of the National Cancer Institute of the National Institutes of Health.

In his introduction to the hearing, Representative Rogers mentioned the thousands of letters of protest from citizens, the new Canadian epidemiological study, and raised the questionable scientific quality of the FDA's decision-making. He emphasized that the hearing was to reconsider both the scientific evidence on saccharin and the proposed ban. Most members of the Subcommittee focused on the scientific rigor of the new Canadian study as a justification for the FDA ban (Ibid.:1–3).

The following excerpts from the questioning between Representative Rogers and Dr. Kennedy of the FDA show how the legislator cast doubt on the new evidence throughout the hearing (Ibid.: 54–55). Both interchanges are taken from the hearing record. In the first, Representative Rogers asked Kennedy if the Canadian study could be "invalid" (see the dialogues that follow). To suggest significant doubt was a powerful starting point. Kennedy from the FDA responded that the agency had requested evaluations of the Canadian study by epidemiologists in and outside of the organization. If some scientist could justify why the Canadian findings should not be considered, then the FDA would listen.

He emphasized that the FDA was playing an "open-minded" role in the assessment of scientific findings.

The second dialogue excerpt gives a more extended view of the exchange between Rogers and Dr. Kennedy. In this instance, Rogers tried to get Dr. Kennedy to agree that the Canadian study had "problems" or "deficiencies." Rogers also tried to blame Dr. Kennedy for not being a neutral expert because he favored the Canadian study over other studies. And at the end of the interchange, Rogers even implied that Dr. Kennedy was fabricating evidence by denying what the Canadian study claimed in its report. These exchanges between Rogers and Dr. Kennedy were debates on the science more than were earlier questions and answer between Senator Kennedy and the scientists in the Senate's hearing.

Analysis of Hearing in House of Representatives (key phrases italicized by author for emphasis)

Rogers: "Can you think of any reason why the Canadian study might be considered *invalid*?"

Dr. Kennedy: "Mr. Chairman, the epidemiologists we have asked to evaluate the Canadian study include *some inside and some outside the FDA*. . . .They pronounce it superior . . . to the smaller studies that produce negative results, and as a sensitive conclusion . . . one would have to give the preponderance of the evidence to that study. . . .We want the American *Scientific Community to have a chance to evaluate it*. . . . It may be that *somebody much smarter* than any of us finds a reason why we shouldn't pay any attention to it, and *if they can produce a convincing argument, surely we will listen to it*."

Rogers: "I think the Canadian study said they had *problems*, did it not? They even admitted that in their report."

Dr. Kennedy: "Everyone we have asked about it, Mr. Chairman, believes the Canadian study to be superior to [that] previously published."

Rogers: "I said didn't they actually say that there were many discrepancies between cases and controls that can have an effect on the outcome?"

Dr. Kennedy: "They simply said that they had not as yet produced a complete tabulation of their comparisons between cases and controls with respect to all other variables."

Rogers: "I am talking about the *deficiencies* in this study, not other studies."

Dr. Kennedy: "Mr. Chairman, it is quite possible there are deficiencies in this study."

Rogers: "I don't know why you don't want to say it is a deficiency when they have not done a proper study of the record of bladder and kidney infections. *Why do you defend this and not others*?"

Dr. Kennedy: "Mr. Chairman, I repeat that it is in the view of our epidemiologist and my own view that these deficiencies are less serious than the deficiencies in the other studies mentioned."

Rogers: *"Is there a deficiency in the Canadian study, when they themselves tell us that there is a deficiency in the study?"*

Dr. Kennedy: "Did they use the word 'deficiency'"?

Rogers: "Examination."

[*Note*: All testimony from pp. 54–55 of the hearing.]

The barrage of questions for the head of the FDA was sufficient to leave the ban on shaky scientific grounds in the minds of congresspersons.

In November 1977 Congress proposed legislation that called for a moratorium on the ban until 1979, the institution of warning labels, and further testing. Both the House of Representatives and the Senate approved it on November 4, and President Carter signed the law on November 23. This law was entitled The Saccharin Study and Labeling Act of 1977.

This "Saccharin Moratorium" required all manufacturers of saccharin to place warnings on their products that the artificial sweetener might cause cancer in humans. The move preserved the market for saccharin in all existing sugar-free foods, beverages, cosmetics, and drugs. The act also asked the NAS to investigate whether the risk of human cancer could be extrapolated from evidence of bladder tumors in test animals. The NAS was instructed to recommend legislative and administrative actions, and to evaluate federal regulatory policy for food additives in general. The regulatory role to the FDA was thus withdrawn by the Congress.

Congress found in this case of saccharin regulations that it could not live with the consequences of its own Delaney Clause. It therefore passed another law eliminating saccharin from the rule of Delaney. This is unusual, but not unprecedented. Brooks (personal comments 7/11/89) notes a similar instance when Congress repealed an Environmental Impact Statement requirement for the Alaska pipeline during the energy crisis of 1979. Both of these are cases of congressional withdrawals of the authority delegated to regulatory agencies (Brooks, personal comments, 7/11/89: 10).

Nevertheless, the Food, Drugs and Cosmetics Act was never eliminated as a permanent U.S. law. Every two years the Saccharin Moratorium has been routinely extended, keeping the artificial sweetener out of reach of the FDA. In effect, Congress has superseded the authority of the FDA to regulate saccharin.

Allan Mazur (1981) has pointed out such rhetorical and polemic strategies that experts use to deal with disputes over scientific evidence. He notes that experts often question or deny the existence of contrary evidence posed by opponents. Or experts faced with ambiguous data and theories can use several typical strategies to argue their points. They may reject conflicting data, propose alternative interpretations, and take opposing positions when any of several polar positions would be reasonable. Mazur (1981: 14–18, 20–29) has demonstrated these strategies in issues of both low-level radiation from nuclear power plants and water fluoridation.

Here I extend this argument to encompass the role of legislators. Legislators are even more powerful than experts. They are in a position to assess for government whether an agency's interpretation of scientific uncertainty is justifiable or should be revised. Given this important role, it is clear why Congress can use science to condemn an agency's performance.

Scientific Uncertainty. Several of the political strategies for challenging scientific uncertainty arose in the saccharin hearings of the Senate and House Subcommittees. In particular, the key strategies included Doubtful Extrapolation, Inadequate Data Base, and Disputed Explanation. Although the extrapolation challenge does not appear in the interchanges here, it did play an important role in the critique that legislators launched at the FDA and its proposed ban.

The strategies were aimed to shift the burden of proof. The Delaney Clause had given manufacturers the responsibility to prove saccharin's lack of carcinogenicity. The FDA had to show one experiment of cancer induction in rats to justify a ban of manufacturing of the sweetener. Congress, therefore, used the Subcommittee hearings to erode this evidence of saccharin's carcinogenicity, implicate its impurities, and argue that such uncertain findings could not be claimed. By splitting their vote, scientists showed how impartial they were to a political shift in the burden of proof. Congress could withdraw its delegation of authority from the agency. It could also transform its conviction so that potential opponents, *not* manufacturers, would be responsible for proving carcinogenicity, subject to legal or legislative safeguards. This would shift the burden of proof from manufacturers to potential opponents of saccharin.

In the Senate hearing, Senators Kennedy and Schweiker coordinated the attack. Senator Kennedy was initially receptive to the idea of saccharin being a human carcinogen. Senator Schweiker, however, launched a relentless barrage of questions that built hypotheses using the uncertain findings of scientists. By the end of the interrogation, no one was surprised to find saccharin nearly freed of carcinogenic suspicion. The hypothetical findings had built confidence in senators that the impurities associated with saccharin, and not saccharin itself, were the true carcinogens.

The criticism of research protocol in collecting data occurred in the hearing of the House of Representatives. Representative Rogers aggressively eroded confidence in the new Canadian study of the epidemiology of saccharin, which was one of the two large and new researches on humans in 1977. Instead of supporting the new research, Rogers used a three-pronged attack of undermine its implication that saccharin was carcinogenic. The first aim was to downgrade the validity of the epidemiological data in the study. Second, Rogers insisted that the relationship between cases and controls had been poorly supervised. Third, Rogers claimed that the Canadian study had criticized its own methodology.

Senator Schweiker also insisted that the FDA had used a misguided explanation of the epidemiological results. This was basically an attempt to shift the explanation for the finding of carcinogenicity from saccharin itself to the impurities resulting from its manufacture. This is of doubtful relevance unless a manufacturing process that eliminates impurities can be guaranteed. Still, Schweiker submitted several feasible hypotheses for why impurities could instead be the real carcinogens.

Bargaining Analysis. A bargaining analysis of this saccharin case (see Figure 3) demonstrates the role of the outside option. The FDA offered its decision to ban saccharin, the citizens (diabetics and dieters) and diet-drink industry rejected the offer and introduced the legislature as their outside option. Congress reversed the FDA decision by recasting the scientific evidence on saccharin carcinogenicity.

The primary focus of this case was to shift the burden of proof from manufacturers of saccharin to opponents of its use. The Delaney Clause specified that only one experiment had to demonstrate carcinogenicity. The FDA assumed, therefore, that the manufacturer would take the responsibility to prove his product was not carcinogenic. But Congress introduced an alternative position on the burden of proof. It decided that manufacturers could be relatively free of restraint, and instead placed the responsibility on future opponents to prove that products were not safe. The final bargain was that Congress withdrew the agency's authority to regulate saccharin.

Congressional Dominance. In order to explain the power of congressional subcommittees over regulatory agencies, we need a model of congressional control. Such a model, "Congressional Dominance," has been developed by Weingast (1984) and Weingast and Moran (1983,

Figure 3
Saccharin Bargaining

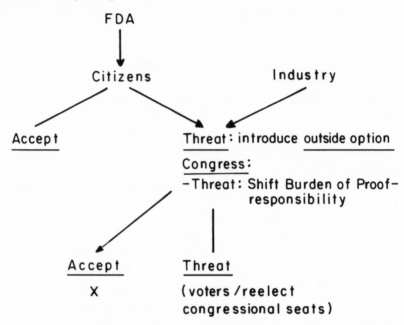

1986a). It represents a new theory of bureaucratic behavior, which grows out of the rational choice theory of public policy (Shepsle 1978; Romer and Rosenthal 1978). The fundamental assumption is that the traditional model of regulatory autonomy (Niskanen 1971, 1975) no longer holds, particularly when congressional committees start to supervise regulatory decisions. This is clearly the case in the saccharin study we have just reviewed. Congress had the power of a supervisor throughout the relationship between agency and congressional committee.

Legislators control bureaucrats through an incentive system of rewards and sanctions, which exists even though the agency has a statute. Congress rewards those agencies that pursue policies of interest to Congress and sanction those agencies that refuse to give support. If this incentive system works effectively, agencies pursue congressional goals. The danger signals for Congress are when citizens complain. Citizens act as the constituents of Congress.

Public hearing like those for saccharin are asset-intensive activities. They are used only when an agency like the FDA is functioning in a questionable manner. It is arguable that the FDA was merely following congressional intent as expressed in the Delaney Clause. The problem was that Congress did not like the logical consequences of its own prescription for saccharin. The implementation of legislation, even by an expert agency like the FDA, can expose logical inconsistencies in congressional judgments. In fact, the Delaney Clause is actually unenforceable across the board since it would ban table salt, which produces cancer in mice if ingested in sufficient quantities.

The key aspects in the incentive system are sanctions for erring agencies, budgetary favors, and appointments of agency leadership. Oversight comes from new legislation, like the Saccharin Moratorium, which limits agency behavior. The fundamental interest of all legislators is to maximize political and electoral support from home districts (Weingast and Moran 1983: 768-769).

The key means to guarantee district support is through the committee system of Congress. Legislators choose to be on committees that serve their own constituencies (Shepsle 1978). Senator Kennedy may have decided that the Subcommittee on Health and Scientific Research focused on the issues about which his electors, both citizens and industrialists in Massachusetts, would be most concerned. For saccharin, this meant diabetics, dieters, and the diet-drink industry. He could gain leverage over industrial control and health regulation, which he may have judged to be a critical aspect of his own political support and reelection. Such committees have near monopolies over the small set of issues they treat. They can make proposals, which will be approved subject to majority rule of the entire legislature. Or, they can veto proposals made by other groups.

The important consequence of this is that specific oversight committees like that of Senator Kennedy may have more control over a particular agency like the FDA than does the rest of Congress (Weingast and Moran 1983: 771-772). Regardless of the agency's mandate, the committee can reward an agency that pursues a regulatory strategy that conforms to the political interests of committee members.

Weingast and Moran (1983) predict several types of regulatory outcomes based on the premise that Congress can control agency behavior. First, members of a congressional committee can insulate an agency from the influence of members of Congress not on the committee. Second, if members of the committee remain over a long period, the regulatory policy of the agency will tend to be stable. Oversight committees become the most important determinants of decision change. And finally, agencies like the FDA that pursue regulations against the interests of congressional committees are likely to suffer from congressional sanctions like the Saccharin Moratorium (Weingast and Moran 1983: 774–775).

Scientific uncertainty is clearly used as a political rationale. Both Senator Kennedy and Representative Rogers wanted a market-based regulation to replace the government ban proposed by the FDA. Both Kennedy, assisted by Senator Schweiker, and Rogers used the uncertainty prevalent in the saccharin research to undermine any scientific conviction that the ban was necessary.

When analyzed as relationships between the legislator and bureaucrat, however, several important factors may be overlooked. First, the bureaucrat has his or her own interests and makes decisions based on information not entirely available to legislators. There is no guarantee, therefore, that a substantial amount of "slippage" may not occur between what the legislator wants and the bureaucratic performance he gets. Second, the relationship is not just a bargain between one legislator and one bureaucrat. It is, instead, several government bodies competing to influence the bureaucrat. These bodies may include the Office of Management and Budget, the president, and other departmental units in the executive branch. Finally, agency oversight may be lodged in committees that do not determine the vote of Congress. When votes occur, therefore, the committee cannot be sure that the majority will favor the recommendation of the committee (Moe 1987: 480–483). How does the bargain struck in the saccharin case compare with that in the dioxin case?

The Dioxin Case

In August 1985 the New York City Board of Estimate held its public hearing. It adopted the FEIS and positive recommendations of the City Planning Commission about the siting decision. This authorized the DOS to enter into a contract with a selected vendor. The residents of Brooklyn took the case to the Supreme Court of Kings County to appeal to the judge to prevent the incinerator. The BOE was the defendant (although the DOS was actually the agency in charge of the decisions made). The following case analysis examines two court decisions between November 1985 and July 1986 (Schiff et al. v. BOE et al., NY Supreme Court 1985; Schiff et al. v. BOE et al., Appellate Division 1986—hereafter referred to as Schiff v. BOE 1985 or 1986)

On November 26, 1985, the Kings County Supreme Court ordered that a trial be held on the issues raised by nine Brooklyn and Manhattan residents (Schiff v. BOE 1985). Their appeal concerned the inadequacy of the FEIS prepared by the DOS. Specifically, the residents claimed that the FEIS inadequately discussed projected amounts of dioxin emissions, dangers of toxic and explosive waste in the incinerator, the method of site selection, and problems of ash disposal, noise, odor, and water quality. The residents alleged that the Board of Estimate had acted in an arbitrary and capricious manner by approving the incinerator (Environmental Defense Fund v. Flacke 1983). Special Term decided that these complaints were issues of fact that should be treated in a trial with expert testimony (Schiff v. BOE 1986: 1–2).

The three main issues of fact concerned the scientific evidence used to select data, disregard other data, and protect health. Specifically, the residents referred to the insufficient data base in the FEIS, the inadequate disclosure of "valid alternative possibilities for higher dioxin emission," and the inadequate standards that failed to reflect the effect of dioxin emissions on human health (Petitioners' Answer, Schiff v. BOE 1985). These three points claimed that the FEIS did not present a "hard look" at environmental effects and a "reasoned elaboration" upon which the Board of Estimate could base its decision.

The first point focused on whether disagreement among scientists over data must be examined in the FEIS. Residents claimed that although such disagreements "need not be resolved, they *must* be fairly explained." A decisionmaker could not assess the worth of a proposal in an "unbiased fashion" if differing views of experts were not also taken into consideration. Moreover, the residents emphasized that the examination of differing views must occur in the FEIS, not in other hearings and conferences which the DOS attended.

The court had authority to demand answers to two key questions regarding the scientific uncertainty about data used in the case. First, if the DOS could not know with any scientific certainty what the environmental effects would be, did the DOS outline the full range of potential adverse environmental effects? Second, did the FEIS inform the public and decisionmakers what would happen if the preferred theories of the DOS were incorrect (Petitioners' Answer, Ibid.: 9)? If the FEIS did not answer these two questions, then the BOE could not make a rational decision according to the requirements of either SEQRA or the burden of proof.

Another criticism was in the choice of emissions rate for dioxin used in the FEIS. Residents contended that the use of a single test performed at the Chicago-Northwest facility during 1980 was insufficient data to estimate the emissions rate. This was particularly true given "no scientific consensus" that dioxin is formed and regulated by controlling both temperature and combustion in the incinerator.

On this point, two dioxin experts who peer-reviewed the Hart Report criticized the single-test assumption (Petitioners' Answer, Ibid.: 13–14). Dr. Hutzinger insisted that there were no sound data to indicate that the proposed incinerator would emit less PCDD or PCDF than another design run under optimal conditions (Hart 1984: App. D, Hutzinger comments). Dr. Goldfarb also pointed out that extreme uncertainty exists in the tests from various international incinerators. He said "it is thus likely that the [incinerator] will emit dioxin and furan at rates that could easily be ten times, or more, higher than those used in the Hart study and the DEIS" (Affidavit of Dr. Theodore Goldfarb, Schiff v. BOE 1985).

The second point concerned whether the FEIS adequately disclosed valid alternatives for higher dioxin emissions. Dr. Goldfarb said that a group of scientists had indicated to the BOE that since the components of municipal solid waste were sufficiently unknown, no scientists could determine dioxin or furan levels (Ibid.).

The final point raised by the residents concerned inadequate health standards. Given the scientific uncertainties in the calculations of dose-response relationships of dioxin, residents criticized the FEIS for discussing standards without pointing out limitations. For example, standards failed to account for the carcinogenic nature of dioxins and furans other than 2,3,7,8-TCDD (Petitioners' Memorandum, Ibid.).

On April 3, 1986, the Appellate Division reversed the order of the lower Supreme Court, and the proceeding was dismissed (Schiff v. BOE 1986). The reasoning of the four judges of the Appellate Division was that nothing in the SEQRA required an agency to come to a particular decision on any issue. Moreover, they decided that the legislature had intentionally given the agency "considerable latitude" in evaluating environmental effects and in making decisions. The court's role, the judges concluded, was merely to assure that the agency had satisfied the SEQRA procedurally and substantively. An EIS would pass judicial scrutiny if it identified areas of environmental concern, took a "hard look" at them, and made a "reasoned elaboration" in reaching a decision (Jackson v. New York State Urban Development Corporation 1986).

The judges of the Appellate Court therefore determined that a Special Term was not warranted. The FEIS was sufficient. The judges pointed out that the FEIS did not have to demonstrate "scientific unanimity" on the desirability of a proposed action (Environmental Defense Fund v. Flacke 1983:3).

According to the lawyers for the BOE, the faulty contention of the petitioners was that disagreement among scientists represented a litigable claim in court. The BOE claimed that mere existence of scientific disagreement was no cause of action when assessing compliance with environmental disclosure requirements (Respondents' Position, Schiff v. BOE 1985: 1–2). The lawyers for the BOE stated that the presence of uncertainty was not reason to overturn decisions made by government officials with the authority to make them. Moreover, the legislature did not want the court to resolve disputed scientific theories raised by supporters or opponents of a public decision. Thus, the lawyers of the BOE stated that the court should be "deferential" to the regulatory agency in such circumstances (Respondents' Position, Ibid.: 18–19).

Lawyers of the BOE also stated that the procedure of risk assessment is fundamental to understanding the legitimacy of agency assumptions and calculations. As indicated in the Hart Report, risk assessment attempts to link health risk with a worst case or upper bound of risk. Actual risks are likely to be much lower than the worst-case risk estimate (Hart 1984: 5–37). The key point of the BOE was that while the assumptions and uncertainties associated with risk estimates should be made public, the "potential for deriving a different number under a different set of assumptions is simply irrelevant" (Respondents' Position, Schiff v. BOE 1985: 9). Thus, the risk assessment was judged by the depth of the analysis, the presentation of assumptions and uncertainties, and the articulation of various points of view. The assessment of risk, however, was *not* measured by "whether all those who commented upon it agree with each of the underlying assumptions" (Ibid.: 10).

In conclusion, the two courts agreed on who had responsibility: the citizens. But the courts were diametrically opposed on the level of the standard at which to place the burden of proof in the incinerator case. The Supreme Court of Kings County was willing to overturn the regulatory agency by insisting that the full range of scientific disagreement over the dioxin issues must be represented in the FEIS. This would introduce the risk that citizens had analyzed, with the help of Commoner, as a standard of necessary risk. But the Appellate Division reversed this position. It instead claimed that the position of the court should be one of deference to the regulatory agencies. The Appellate Division therefore insisted that the agencies should determine on their own which scientists, which assumptions, and which uncertainties should appear in their assessments of risk. Accordingly, the agency could determine that the necessary standard had not yet been reached. Can we interpret this case evidence as an example of the power of courts to overturn or reinforce decisions made in the presence of scientific doubt?

Scientific Uncertainty. In the dioxin case, the two courts split over whether to tolerate or eliminate scientific uncertainty. The judge in the lower Supreme Court of New York State decided to challenge the proposal of the DOS to site the incinerator. The judge rejected the agency's use of Disputed Parameter Values, Inadequate Data Base, Disputed Explanation, and Challenged Regulation of Uncertainty. But when the case was reconsidered in the higher Appellate Division of New York State, the four judges simply eliminated scientific uncertainty as evidence, and used a legal justification to favor the agency's decision. We review the two court cases separately here.

In the lower Supreme Court, the judge insisted that the data base be carefully examined. Variability in the data and scientific disputes over data were chief concerns. The judge also demanded that all factors contributing to uncertainty be fully reported. This meant an examination of the complete range of possible health effects. This included noise, odor, water quality, as well as carcinogenic effects of dioxin emissions. The judge asked that regulations be in place to protect the public. These could take the form of public information as well as protective restrictions on ambient levels of contaminants in the locality.

A key strategy was to challenge the sufficiency of the agency's data sample. The number of incinerators was too few to assess dioxin emission rates. Only one set of measurements at the Chicago-Northwest incinerator was used, augmented by some data from a Swiss plant. In the peer-review, one of the experts noted that emission rates of dioxins and furans at most plants had been tens to thousands of times higher than those at either the Chicago or Swiss plant. He argued that the formation of dioxin or furan is insufficiently understood to ignore measurements from plants just because they do not have Martin-type furnaces like the proposed Brooklyn plant (Petitioners' Answer, Schiff v. BOE 1985: 16). Moreover, the EPA had recorded very high emission rates in Virginia (10 to 100 times over Chicago's rate) (Goldfarb, Schiff v. BOE 1985).

Another aspect of data insufficiency concerned the lack of a comprehensive review of research on adverse effects. The FEIS, according to citizens, analyzed only a very limited range of environmental and health effects. The carcinogenic effect of dioxin exposure was treated indirectly by referring to the study by Hart. The FEIS claimed, according to the citizens and the lower court, that additional effects like health issues, odor, and noise were rare.

A third challenge of scientific uncertainty concerned the disputed explanations of emission measurements that were used by the agency. Scientific consensus is lacking on how dioxin was formed according to temperature, combustion efficiency, and location in the incinerator. Some scientists argue that dioxin may be produced in the cooler areas of the incineration system such as the air pollution control devices or smoke-stack. If this were true, then the FEIS would be incorrect in claiming that high temperatures and efficient combustion would reduce dioxin emissions. These effects would occur prior to dioxin formation. This uncertain interpretation of the scientific information must be acknowl-edged by decisionmakers. According to one expert, Dr. Goldfarb, the mechanism of dioxin formation and destruction is so uncertain that several alternative scientific hypotheses exist but have not been verified to explain it. Although chemical reactivity and thermal stability *suggest* that high temperatures can control dioxin and furan emissions, no proof of this (as far as I know) has yet been achieved for the complex and variable mixture of materials in municipal solid waste. This was the "clear consensus" of scientists and engineers who met at the New York Academy of Sciences to inform the BOE of the state of scientific knowledge about municipal waste incineration (Goldfarb, Schiff v. BOE 1985.).

The final strategy challenged the regulation of uncertainty. What would happen if the rate of dioxin emissions went higher than expected? No information was accessible to the public to explain the possible adverse health and environmental impacts if the theories used by the agency proved to be wrong. Moreover, there were only inadequate health standards in place to protect the public if exposure levels of dioxin did start to become unsafe. Only one compound of dioxin, but not all dioxins and furans, was limited through a guideline on its ambient concentration.

The lower Supreme Court thus determined that the scientific evidence was insufficient for the FEIS to claim that the level of health risk was "negligible." The data on dioxin emission rates from incinerators were sparse. The treatment of adverse carcinogenic effects was minimal in the FEIS and the explanation of formation and destruction of dioxin com-pounds was inadequate. Finally, the FEIS did not address the problem of how to regulate uncertainty if dioxin emission rates became too high and the health standards remained insufficient. Thus, the judge claimed that the evidence was much too uncertain. A new trial was needed to introduce more scientific evidence, to improve public understanding of the level of health risk, and to decide whether the incinerator should be sited at all.

When the decision came to the Appellate Division, however, the leading judge took a contrary position. He decided that an end could be placed on the search for scientific evidence. This would protect the agency's authority to make decisions.

This leading judge took a deferential role toward the agency as decisionmaker. The purpose of the court was not to reverse decisions, but instead to affirm agency prerogative in facing uncertainty. The judge agreed that requiring consideration of the full range of scientific uncertainty was too great a demand to make of an agency. The judge also affirmed that risk assessment was a technically adequate method with which to analyze health risk. It was specific rather than general, made limited assumptions, and specified uncertainties. All of these aspects of risk assessment were to be determined in-house by the agency bureaucrat responsible for the decision.

In sum, the judge clarified that the court should defer to agencies as the proper decisionmakers. This was specified by the regulatory laws and enforced by the legislature. The courts are neither entitled nor equipped to resolve disputed scientific theories of opponents or proponents of regulatory decisions. Nor are the courts supposed to relitigate technical issues that should be examined in an administrative forum. Instead, judges should defer to decisionmakers unless the record shows a clear failure to observe due process. This is particularly true when agencies are utilizing their special expertise in risk assessment at the frontiers of current science.

The judge's decision did address the strategy used by the judge of the lower Supreme Court to argue that insufficient data was used (Inadequate Data Base). He completely validated the agency's use of only partial information. The position of the judge was that SEQRA did not require a comprehensive review of health effects. Moreover, although decisionmakers should be aware of scientific disagreement, they are not required to change their decision because of it. Let us review these judicial defenses of a limited data base in decision-making.

The judge first clarified that SEQRA requires the agency to take a "hard look" and make a "reasoned elaboration" of environmental impacts. The agency must disclose not all but only significant impacts that can be "reasonably anticipated." Moreover, the agency should make project decisions that are "analytical and not encyclopedic." Furthermore, the "hard look" standard does not require the agency to analyze *de novo* every environmental impact in the FEIS. SEQRA allows an agency considerable latitude in assessing a proposed project, and encourages discretion in determining appropriate results and relevant evidence (Respondents' Supplementary Memorandum, Schiff v. BOE 1985: 13–15).

The judge also recognized that risk assessment is a common regulatory strategy to reduce scientific uncertainty. The method specifies parameters and quantifies the risk expected from the decisions. This risk estimate can then be compared with quantified risks of other decisions. The agency can use its scientists to make necessary assumptions and to identify unavoidable uncertainties. But every scientist outside the agency does not need to agree with these assumptions or uncertainties. That would be unrealistic and nearly impossible given that there is so much disagreement among scientists doing research.

The judge leading agreed that scientific disagreement was acceptable. Such disagreement would not invalidate an EIS. The purpose of the EIS is to inform decisionmakers of the implications of a project, regardless of the amount of uncertainty (Ibid.: 18).

By contrast to the lower Supreme Court, the judges of the Appellate Division determined that the burden of proof was satisfactory. The existing review of scientific evidence in the FEIS was sufficient to demonstrate that a high standard of proof had not yet been met by the citizens. According to the judges, an end could be placed on the search for both scientific evidence and scientific unanimity. Besides, agencies had the right to make decisions no matter how uncertain or sparse the evidence. Risk assessment provides an adequate methodology. Finally, courts were not entitled or equipped to make scientific decisions for agencies. The judges therefore claimed that the scientific evidence was sufficient. The health risk would remain minimal, and the incinerator could be sited in Brooklyn.

Bargaining Analysis. A bargaining analysis of the dioxin case (see Figure 4) demonstrates the role of the outside option. The DOS (sponsored by the BOE) offered its decision to site the incinerator. The Brooklyn residents rejected the offer and introduced their outside option—the lower Supreme Court. This court threatened the DOS by claiming that the agency had inadequately treated the scientific uncertainty on risk level. The DOS then introduced its own outside option—the higher Appellate Division. This court rejected the lower court's claim, and insisted that the existing FEIS did sufficiently analyze the risk level. The decision, therefore, would *not* change.

Different from the saccharin case, the focus of the dioxin case was on adjusting the standard of proof. The responsibility remained with the citizens to prove that dioxin was carcinogenic. But all groups questioned at what standard of proof a decision would be made. If the proof had to be at a low standard, the siting would not occur. If the proof was at a high standard, however, the siting would take place. Both bargains occurred, but the second one overruled the legal validity of the first.

Judicial Review. The discussion of the dioxin case reflects a dispute over "substantive evidence" and "procedural evidence." Judge

Figure 4
Dioxin Bargaining

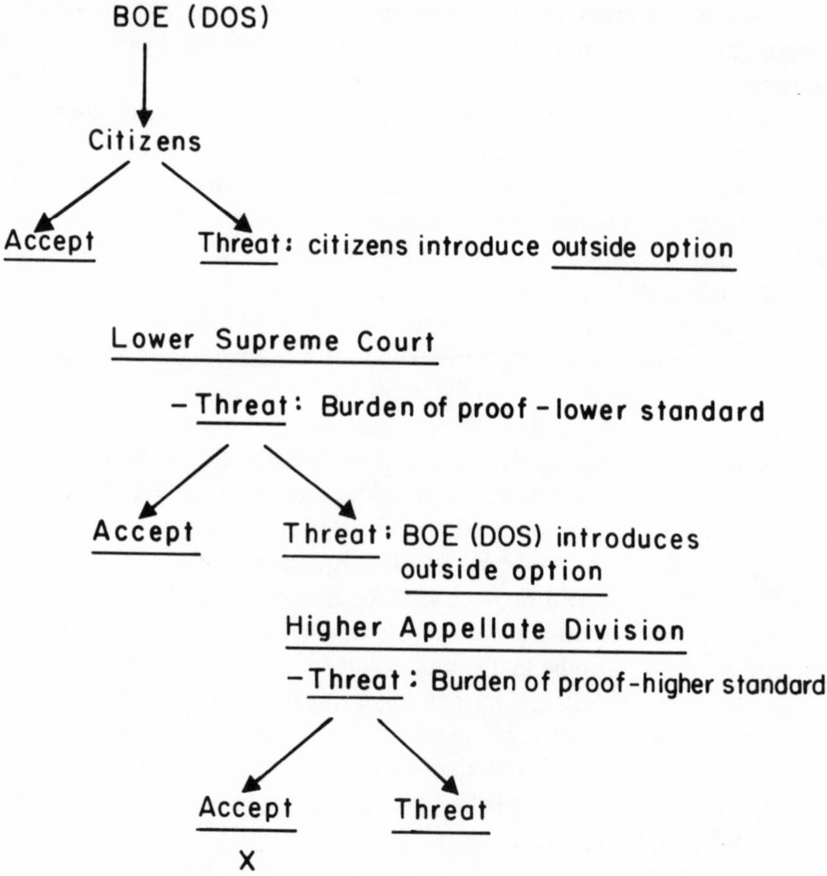

BOE (DOS)

Citizens

Accept   Threat: citizens introduce outside option

Lower Supreme Court

－Threat: Burden of proof - lower standard

Accept   Threat: BOE (DOS) introduces
                       outside option

Higher Appellate Division

－Threat : Burden of proof - higher standard

Accept   Threat

X

Leventhal (1974) has suggested that "substantive evidence" should define what is needed to support a finding of fact. "Arbitrary and capricious" evidence should examine the agency's transition from facts to conclusions. The following is a short excursion into only some of the legal issues.

Substantive evidence is consistent with the typical understanding of what constitutes a rational and thorough review required in a "hard look." According to Judge Leventhal a "hard look" requires that assumptions be spelled out, inconsistencies explained, contrary evidence rebutted, guesswork eliminated, and conclusions supported. Some effort to do each of these can be made by an agency. If a great extent of scientific uncertainty is generated in the effort, it can detract from the quality of the report. The agency may claim that it has taken a "hard look," yet residents may also claim that the look was out of focus. In their claim of insufficient data and inadequate disclosures of high emissions rates, the Brooklyn residents directly criticized the DOS's treatment of scientific uncertainty.

According to Judge Bazelon (1981:212), it is essential to disclose any uncertainty that weakens a decision. This uncertainty includes both the "agency's ignorance as well as its quantitative estimates of error." His argument is that disclosure of uncertainty can improve the quality of the information in the decision by revealing weaknesses early on. Peer review, oversight by the legislature, and examination by citizens can bolster the substance of the decision.

Judges are able, according to Judge Leventhal, to acquire the necessary technical knowledge. This enables them to review whether the agency has completed a substantial investigation as required by Section 706 of the Administrative Procedures Act. Courts should strike down decisions when they reflect "arbitrary and capricious" procedures to reach a decision.

Only rarely, according to Abraham and Merrill (1986), does a judge actually decide to enter the scientific merits of the data presented. This means that the judge will confront the uncertainties treated by the agency and try to reinterpret the findings. Given that truth cannot be decided given such uncertainties, Abraham and Merrill (1986: 94) argue this leads to difficult political dilemmas in decision-making that judges prefer to avoid.

In the dioxin case, however, decisions of the agency and the Appellate Division disregarded this cautious viewpoint. The agency appeared quite indifferent to the substantial amount of disagreement over the dioxin emission rates. The DOS even determined that a risk of slightly *over* the *de minimis* level (one cancer case per million people exposed to dioxin emissions) was acceptable in order to build the incinerator.

The Appellate Division agreed with this disinterested assessment of risks. The FEIS was not "insufficient" solely because citizens disputed the evidence and scientists disagreed about the findings. Nor was the FEIS "insufficient" just because the lower Supreme Court had approved citizen claims against actions of the agency. The Appellate Court also insisted that it could not "second guess" the DOS's choice of decision. Second-guessing means that the court reinterprets both the meaning of agency statutes and the evidence upon which agencies formulate their decisions.

By contrast, Judge Bazelon (1981) argues that such a substantive review of the technical evidence and assumptions can actually be replaced by a simple review of agency procedures. This detour from substance to procedure avoids the court's need to "second-guess" the agency. It also seems to side-step the responsibility and technical capacity, however, to resolve scientific uncertainties.

Legal scholars like Shep Melnick (1983) claim that judges in such situations prefer that agencies make the factual conclusion and policy choices. This leaves the judges merely to supervise procedures. Judges feel unprepared to make public decisions in technical matters, and they have no technical knowledge to resolve controversies. According to Melnick (1983:60) judges realize that they are safer when free from technical uncertainties in which there is no truth. Otherwise, justices would have to make decisions on what Judge Bazelon calls "homespun scientific aphorisms."

According to Abraham and Merrill (1986:94), most courts prefer to "defer" to an agency's decision. They simply defer to the regulatory agency that has jurisdiction to request a scientific analysis and make a decision. According to these authors, judges can also decide to "avoid" a decision by reformulating a dispute. Although they may not want to resolve the scientific problem, judges may know of some other statutory basis upon which they can resolve a controversy.

HYPOTHESIS

I assume that scientific evidence is highly uncertain in all three cases. The saccharin case involved data and extrapolation uncertainties that exacerbated controversies over the level of health risk. The dioxin case focused on both parameter and data uncertainties that also caused disagreement over the level of risk. And the LNG case involved model uncertainties that threw doubt on the number of people at risk.

This book suggests causes of change in regulatory decisions. I argue that decisions change when citizens or industrialists protest (Chapter 3) and supreme outside options (legislature or highest court) take scientific uncertainty into account (Chapter 4). Scientific challenges in the absence of strong citizen opposition are ineffective in changing regulatory decisions. This was demonstrated in the LNG case. In the presence of strong citizen opposition, scientific uncertainty becomes an important political resource. Citizens or industrialists can change a decision, however, only by relying on the superior authority of the legislature or court to use scientific uncertainty to shift the burden of proof. This was demonstrated in the dioxin and saccharin cases.

Chapter 5 compares European cases with U.S. cases of legislative and judicial challenges of uncertain science. To what extent do different structures of government and relations with experts, citizens, or industrialists affect whether scientific issues remain central?

Chapter Five

National Comparisons

How does the argument in this book compare with those of others in the study of regulatory institution? Some scholars focus on bargaining in government, some on bureaucratic administration, and some on pluralist interpretations of leadership. This chapter contrasts these various interpretations of governmental behavior with my own to identify consensus and controversy in understanding the politics of scientific uncertainty.

First, I review the contribution of this book to the study of the U.S. government as a regulatory institution. The resulting model is then applied to examine European governments. My conclusion interprets the divergence between national states in the United States and Europe in terms of the study of regulatory institutions. An Appendix reviews the bargains that occurred in three European and three U.S. cases of public health, technological safety, and environmental quality.

THE GOVERNMENT AS REGULATOR AND BARGAINER

I begin with the premise that many decisions in public health, technological safety, and environmental quality are characterized by substantial degrees of uncertainty about the science of carcinogenic effects. This means that empirical evidence is sparse, models contradictory, and theory inconsistent or incomplete. Analysts of health risk have to gauge probabilities of hazard on their own, since impacts are impossible to determine precisely. Harvey Brooks and Chester Cooper (1987) argue that the resulting "contextual unknowns" leave scientists unaware of policy applications and policy analysts unaware of useful science. Graham, Green, and Roberts (1989) then show that despite expectations to the contrary, gaining more scientific knowledge and research does not necessarily resolve conflict over policy choices by government agencies.

The politics of interest group influence and government pressures occur when scientists introduce these scientific uncertainties and unknowns into the policy arena. Uncertainties offer citizens (environmentalists included) and industrialists opportunities to challenge the scientific basis of protective choices. They also offer the legislature and courts opportunities to actually change regulatory decisions.

This book contributes to understanding the role of scientific uncertainty in disputes among government institutions. This is when reversals of decisions are most likely to occur. Scientists refer to four types of uncertainties in their controversies over the science of hazards. These include questions about data, parameters, models, and extrapolation. Each type of uncertainty offers officials a different opportunity to make political gains through the use of science. Regulators rely on imprecise statutes that leave uncertainties up to their own discretion. But if decisions are contested, then regulators must defend themselves. Legislators and judges rely on six strategies to interpret uncertainties so that regulatory decisions require changes. In this way, legislators and judges keep regulators either on their statutory path, or off that path if it is no longer politically useful.

The book's second contribution is to provide a new bargaining analysis, the Bureaucratic Bargain. This analysis is designed to interpret disputes and bargains among government bodies. Interest groups play catalytic but subordinate roles.

The model derives from the economic work by Fudenberg and Tirole (1983), Sutton (1986), and Roth (1985), and from Terry Moe's (1984, 1987) work on hierarchical public organizations. The economic analyses examine bargaining with complete information and sequential bargaining with incomplete information. They also enable parties to agree on common interests like prices by bargaining with this information. Finally, they assume that exchanges of concessions for threats are possible among parties. Moe's work focuses on relations among bureaucrats, legislators, and citizens in citizen decision-making organizations. He models decisions as interactions between "principals" and "agents," referring, respectively, to citizens and legislators.

The Bureaucratic Bargain is based on the exchange of decision offers, threats or concessions, and final decisions. Bargaining occurs in two stages. The first stage involves the regulatory agency, which tries to gain the agreement of citizens, industrialists, environmentalists, and scientists to its offered decision. The second stage of the bargaining occurs when a dissatisfied party in the first stage decides to introduce a more powerful government body—the legislature or court. This amounts to introducing an "outside option"—a party that has superior authority over decision-making when compared to all other bargaining parties.

Scientific uncertainties are used as political strategies during these bargaining exchanges. In the first stage, relatively weaker interest groups like citizens can use uncertainty as a political resource to bolster their position with the dominant agency. In the second stage, superior parties like the legislature or court use uncertainties as rationales to legitimize their interpretation of the scientific evidence.

In this second stage, the legislature or court can shift the burden of proof of the hazard's carcinogenicity or safety. Responsibility for proof may be moved to another party. Or, the standard of proof may be increased or decreased in strictness to substantiate carcinogenicity or safety.

The dioxin and saccharin cases showed how the courts and legislature can use scientific uncertainty as a rationale and as a means to shift the burden of proof. Although the lower Supreme Court sided with opposing citizens and scientists by decreasing the standard of proof in the dioxin case, the higher Appellate Division supported the agency by reinstating the increased standard of proof. The latter court eliminated the citizen's and scientist's demand for more treatment of scientific uncertainty. This created a Bureaucratic Bargain, but one never agreed to by the citizens.

By contrast, the saccharin case also produced a Bureaucratic Bargain, but one that effectively removed the agency from the legal responsibility of regulating saccharin. Congress sided with the opposing citizens (diabetics and dieters) and with industry against the proposed saccharin ban. It first reinterpreted the uncertain scientific findings so that a higher standard of proof was required to back the ban. Congress than passed a law introducing a market decision that shifted the responsibility of manufacturers over to opposing citizens. Instead of the manufacturers having to prove saccharin safe, now opponents would have to prove saccharin carcinogenic at a high standard.

In the third case, the decision never changed. Residents were not opposed to the expansion of an LNG plant nearby. As a result they never employed Fay's work on the uncertain science. Three different bargains resulted. In one case the decision was postponed (saccharin). In another case, it was reversed (dioxin). In the third case, the decision survived because no outside option ever intervened (LNG). But could this bargaining analysis work in the European cases?

NATIONAL CASE COMPARISONS: EUROPE AND THE UNITED STATES

Could this analysis and interpretation of government as regulator and bargainer apply to European policy decisions as well as those in the United States? This section briefly compares six case studies of herbicide (2,4,5-T) regulations, nuclear power plant siting, and vinyl chloride (VC) regulations (ERL 1986; Badaracco 1985; Brickman et al. 1985). The herbicide and nuclear power plant cases are in Britain and the United States, and the VC cases in France and the United States. The Appendix following the chapter comprises more extensive studies of all of these cases.

Here, I discuss the comparative evidence and sum up the apparently stark contrast in the empirical findings. This contrast suggests that regulatory agencies ruled without interference of scientists in Europe, but those same agencies were opposed or supported by other government branches and scientists in the United States. In comparing the case studies, the stark contrast in findings appears most clearly if I review the three cases in Europe and then differentiate them from the cases in the United States. We will proceed with the herbicide, nuclear power plant, and vinyl chloride cases in that order. European herbicide regulation (plant sitings) and VC regulation appear to demonstrate that regulatory agencies were in charge of decisions, and scientists were not involved in controversies.

British Opposition to Licensing of Herbicide 2,4,5-T

The herbicide Trichlorophenoxyacetic acid (2,4,5-T) exposes British agriculture workers to sickness and miscarriages from contact with compounds of dioxin when sprayed on broad-leafed brush and weeds (Brickman et al. 1985; ERL 1986). In 1979 the government's Advisory Committee on Pesticides (ACP) stated that no epidemiological evidence or animal tests showed danger to the health of workers. They reported this finding to the Ministry of Agriculture, Fisheries and Food (MAFF), which controls the safety and use of pesticides.

Workers in the National Union of Agricultural and Allied Workers (NUAWW) (now amalgamated with the General and Municipal Workers Union) were not satisfied with this regulatory position. They tried to get the ACP to ban 2,4,5-T. When unsuccessful, the NUAAW convinced the umbrella organization for trade unions in Britain, the Trade Unions Congress (TUC), to call for a ban. The workers even persuaded several large industrial consumers of the herbicide to discontinue its use.

Workers could not gain the support of scientists to help document their plight. So in 1980 they published their own manifesto, which indicated how much workers and their families had suffered from sickness and miscarriages. Workers claimed that existing animal experiments and epidemiological studies were insufficient to represent their case. A dispute arose with the ACP over the definition of "proof." Was proof of safety based on a "balance or probabilities," with damage to health the most probable? Or was proof the strength of the correlation between human contact and adverse health effects?

Despite this opposition, the ACP published reports insisting that the herbicide was not a hazard to worker health. They claimed that a conventional bargain would suffice. The ACP emphasized that the epidemiological evidence was not positive; the Committee also claimed that almost no human risk existed at very low levels of worker exposure. This same agency attitude in securing traditional bargains also dominated the siting of a nuclear power plant.

British Opposition to the Siting of the Sizewell B Nuclear Power Plant

The British government was equally responsive to the idea of siting nuclear power plants (O'Riordan 1987; Davies 1987). In 1979 the Conservatives announced the need for a new type of pressurized water reactor (PWR), the kind that had failed at Three Mile Island in the United States. A Public Inquiry was scheduled in 1982 to review the potential health problems from accidental radiation releases, given a siting of the plant at Sizewell in Suffolk County. The design engineers of the government's Central Electricity Generating Board (CEGB) produced both event-tree and fault-tree analyses to deflect several types of potential technical problems.

But interest groups were already strongly opposed to the idea of a nuclear power plant. The major opposition to the plant's safety came from Friends of the Earth, The Town and Country Planning Association (TCPA), and the Greater London Council (GLC) (disbanded in 1986). Some 4,000 letters of concern were sent to the inspector of the Public Inquiry. Interest groups were concerned that the industry was colluding with the government to promote nuclear power in Britain despite technical problems. Moreover, these opponents were troubled that civil servants in government were insufficiently trained to identify technical problems.

The Inquiry reacted by requiring that only technical and not political concerns be reported in the review of the site. This was strategic and essentially eliminated any criticisms that could not be discounted with technical reasoning. This is not to say, however, that the scientific points were not worthy of concern. For instance, Friends of the Earth indicated several shortcomings of the probabilistic risk analysis (PRA) done by the CEGB. The probability of common-mode failure made it unclear whether the plant could meet the criterion of less than 10^{-6} radioactive releases per reactor per year.

The Inquiry simply side-stepped these technical concerns and proceeded to approve the plant site in 1987. Implicitly, the government and its GEGB decided that nuclear power was important enough to Britain to approve projects even though opposed by public interest groups. As in the British herbicides bargain, the British government insisted upon a conventional bargain in which interest groups would simply comply with the regulatory agency. The French, however, were more committed to cooperate with rather than to dominate opponents in their bargains.

Lack of French Opposition to a Standard for Exposure to Vinyl Chloride

The regulations of vinyl chloride show that French agencies were willing to cooperate with private producers and unions before instituting a formal standard through the Ministry of Labor (Badaracco 1985). This means that regulatory agencies remained in charge, as in Britain, but incorporated rather than defied the opposition of interest groups and unions.

Polyvinyl chloride is used to make phonograph records, vinyl flooring, plastic bottles, as well as baby pacifiers. In 1974 the American B.F. Goodrich company announced that some workers in an American VC plant had died from angiosarcoma of the liver. The Association of Producers of Plastic Materials formed a committee to deal with the issue of VC's cancer-causing potential.

At the same time, the government's National Research and Safety Institute and its National Sickness Insurance Fund moved to reduce exposure levels in factories. These two institutions were "quangos," or organizations administered equally by the government, industrialists, and labor unions. In 1975 and 1976 both institutions recommended reductions in exposure levels, eventually to concentrations of zero owing to VC's carcinogenic risk. These recommendations were not legally binding, but cooperation among interested parties was helpful.

Opposition did occur briefly from a communist union, the Confédération Générale du Travail (CGT). Initially the union complained that workers were being treated as guinea pigs and demanded exposure limits of 1 ppm (parts per million) as in the United States. But these demands ceased when the CGT realized that it wanted to reduce VC exposure levels as much as did VC producers. The only disagreement between the workers and industrialists was on what ultimate level was achievable.

There was also a dearth of controversy over the science of carcinogenicity. Apparently industrialists and workers were satisfied that medical data, measurement techniques for recording VC levels, and methods of controlling VC levels were all being studied. Furthermore, an extensive epidemiological review of worker health histories and medical records had commenced. Workers were informed of all research, and industrialists began to install monitoring immediately.

Only in 1980 did the government's Ministry of Labor issue a legally-binding decree on VC standards. It had taken six years to develop acceptable final standards. The Ministry wanted industrialists to see that sufficient analysis, thought, and trials had gone into eventual standards. Since violators could be fined and imprisoned, this was particulary important. The proposed limits on VC concentrations were also evaluated first by an advisory council of industrialists and workers. When the Ministry of Labor issued its requirement of a weekly average exposure level of 1 ppm with specialized adjustments, no one was surprised. The French government thus regulated VC by avoiding any opposition and keeping scientific uncertainties hidden. The bargain left the regulatory Ministry of Labor in charge.

Thus, in all three European cases, regulatory bargains were struck by preserving the rights of the agency over outside options. Scientific uncertainties were kept out of view. The U.S. cases contrasted radically. The same type of herbicide regulation, nuclear power plant siting, and VC regulation are discussed in the United States. Unlike in Europe, two of the cases were challenged in court (herbicides and VC). The nuclear plant site was entirely canceled by opposition groups presenting scientific uncertainty about earthquakes.

American Opposition to Licensing of Herbicide 2,4,5-T

The herbicide 2,4,5-T was one of the earliest agrochemicals regulated by the EPA. The agency decided immediately to suspend the registration of it for uses on forests and rights of way (Brickman et al. 1985; ERL 1986). Dow Chemical Company was irate and took the agency to court on order to defend its rights of registration for the herbicide. The company argued that the regulatory decisions of the EPA were based on insufficient technical evidence.

Both the scientists of EPA and its Scientific Advisory Board of the Rebuttable Presumption Against Regulation (RPAR) process were involved in the contest. Prior to court involvement, the EPA's scientists had carried out a study called Alsea II, which examined the effects of using the herbicide in Oregon's Alsea Basin. The epidemiological study showed a strong correlation between the rate of miscarriage over a six-year period and the use of the herbicide to spray. The results confirmed earlier findings by the president's scientific advisor that laboratory tests on animals had shown birth defects in offspring.

During the lawsuit, EPA's own RPAR process continued to review other uses of the herbicide. RPAR found that the available data including Alsea II did *not* provide sufficient evidence that the herbicide was an immediate or even substantial threat to human health or the environment. The panel recommended that EPA cancel its registration of the herbicide on rice and range lands.

Now the lawsuit by Dow was beginning to make sense. The EPA and Dow began to negotiate an out-of-court settlement. But Dow was losing too much financially to make an ultimate settlement worthwhile. The company's profits could not offset the legal and administrative costs necessary to defend its registration of the herbicide. This undermined regulatory authority even more.

The ultimate bargain was that the EPA was forced by the court to retain its herbicide regulation. Scientific uncertainties of Alsea II had not been sufficient. This was similar to the case in California, where officials tried to site a nuclear power plant.

American Opposition to the Siting of a Nuclear Power Plant at Bodega Head, California

Scientists from an outside governmental body, the U.S. Geological Survey (USGS), coordinated with a consulting geologist for a political activist. The result was that both offered sufficient scientific uncertainties to defeat an agency's decision to site a nuclear power plant. This case is a stark contrast to the British case in which the agency sited the plant without interference from scientists.

In 1963 the Pacific Gas and Electric Company (PGE) presented the Atomic Energy Commission (AEC) with a proposal to site a nuclear reactor at Bodega Head in California. It would be a conventional steam electric generating plant. PGE had the approval of the state Public Utilities Commission (PUC), and needed only a final approval of the AEC for the reactor and site.

Opposition arose, however, over whether the site was safe for a nuclear reactor. The Sierra Club and a Berkeley activist, David Pesonen, contended that nuclear power was *not* a wise alternative. In particular, several factors—Rachel Carson's moving book *Silent Spring*, the rejection of a reactor in Queens, New York, the Free Speech Movement and its associated ideology against nuclear power—all contributed to political sentiments against the proposed reactor.

But more important, the presence of active earthquake faulting at the site suggested that the decision was not wise for scientific reasons. Despite geological studies by PGE showing the site was distant from population centers and located on solid bedrock, it was not clear whether the area was threatened by earthquakes. The site was also west of the San Andreas fault, a major seam in the earth's crust. Initial risk assessments indicated that the reactor plant would meet the AEC's risk guidelines. All incidents triggered by a fault and leading to a release of radiation would be less than one in a hundred million (1×10^{-8}) per reactor per year. The USGS also estimated that a maximum displacement of ground (due to rupture beneath the power plant) would be no more than the required three feet of horizontal movement.

But a major controversy among scientists and engineers occurred over the chances of a fault at or near the site. The USGS had contradictory reports. One report noted that the sand cap above the sugary bedrock had not been disturbed by earthquakes over thousands of years. But another seismology report examined the tremors and strong shaking of a potential earthquake and concluded that the reactor might not survive in a worse-case scenario. Moreover, David Pesonen, the Berkeley activist, hired a consultant geologist who claimed that the site was unsuitable with significant faults area above the bedrock foundations. At the recommendation of the USGS, the site was resurveyed and an active fault was actually found in the terrace sand and gravel down to the bedrock. USGS geologists estimated that it could move 2–11 feet in the future.

By 1964 the AEC had lost faith in the reactor proposal for Bodega Head. The staff wrote in their report: "Enough uncertainties will create a situation in which 'assurance' can no longer be said to be 'reasonable.'" The AEC report concluded that Bodega was not a suitable site given the state of knowledge at that time. Scientific uncertainty about the site had made a positive regulatory bargain impossible.

Thus, while the American reactor was never sited because of uncertainties in the science, the British reactor was sited. It is not clear to what extent the scientific information was different, or simply treated differently in another political context.

American Opposition to a Standard for Exposure to Vinyl Chloride

The controversial nature of the VC debate in the United States is in strong contrast to its treatment in France. In the United States, the highest court upheld the agency and relied on its full treatment of scientific uncertainty, while in France, the agency cooperated with potential opponents and never had to deal with scientific uncertainties in the evidence (Badaracco 1985).

When B.F. Goodrich announced the worker deaths from angiosarcoma of the liver, the Occupational Safety and Health Administration in 1974 implemented an Emergency Temporary Standard (ETS) that workers not be exposed to levels exceeding 50 ppm. This seemed a level of exposure that industry could achieve. Between May and October of 1974, OSHA set a final exposure standard of an average of 1 ppm and a ceiling of 5 ppm.

Industry was furious. Industry studies of epidemiology had not found a statistically significant rise in the number of liver cancer victims among vinyl chloride workers. Moreover, employee health records showed only angiosarcomas of the liver in older workers exposed to higher VC levels in the 1960s.

The Society of the Plastics Industry (SPI) and six companies—including Goodrich, Shell Chemical, and Dow Chemical—sued OSHA in the Second Circuit Court of Appeals in New York. The SPI wanted an average exposure level of 10 ppm by 1976, and was stunned by OSHA's final standard of 1 ppm in 1974.

The workers, however, brought medical evidence in on their side. The AFL-CIO, United Rubber Workers, and the Oil, Chemical and Atomic Workers supported OSHA. A study by the Mount Sinai School of Medicine reported lung infections in 58 percent of Goodyear workers, and brain and lymphatic cancer in those workers that produced VC. The Harvard School of Public Health also issued a study of 161 records of deceased VC workers that indicated 50 percent more deaths had occurred due to brain and liver cancers. Finally, the National Cancer Institute determined that no threshold of exposure existed below which it was "safe" to be exposed to such carcinogens.

The courts decided to uphold OSHA's standard on VC exposure. The Second Circuit Court of New York recognized that the VC hazard was on the "frontiers of scientific knowledge." The court stated that OSHA had a duty to defend the health of workers even when research and risk assessment was "deficient."

The higher Supreme Court of New York State refused to hear the case on appeal. The court stated that scientific uncertainty had already been fully taken into account. There was no reason to change the existing bargain.

Both the U.S. and French industries were compelled to meet regulatory bargains of a 1 ppm exposure level for VC. The U.S. courts upheld the regulatory standard in 1974 while French industrialists had until 1980 to conform to this same standard.

Comparative Case Findings in Europe and the United States

The case findings in Europe are starkly different from those in the United States. In all three European cases, agencies remained in control of bargains. In Britain, regulatory agencies dominated interest groups like trade unions and local citizen groups; in France, they subdued interest groups like industrialists and trade unions while apparently cooperating. Neither the courts nor parliaments (legislature) were ever involved as outside options. Nor did scientific uncertainty ever play a major role as a rationale for government bodies. Scientists remained behind the scenes politically, and never made public the evidence of uncertainties in the scientific information.

In the U.S. cases, the regulatory agency never ruled alone. In VC regulation, the agency retained its decision by being upheld by the highest court; in the herbicide regulations and nuclear power plant siting, the agency lost in defending its decision. Twice the court was involved: once to strike down the herbicide regulation and once to uphold the VC regulation.

Scientific uncertainty was used as a bargaining rationale in two of the U.S. cases. In the herbicide case, the EPA eventually had to support its own RPAR scientists who found health risk evidence insufficient. In the nuclear power plant siting case, the agency in charge had to face the challenge of both geologists at the U.S. Geological Survey and a consultant hired by a political activist in Berkeley. Both treatments of scientific uncertainty were sufficient to change regulatory bargains.

But in the VC case, the highest court decided that the regulatory decision did not need to change. Scientific uncertainty had already been treated sufficiently in OSHA's initial decision. The independent scientific reports from both Mount Sinai School of Medicine and the Harvard School of Public Health were used to support this finding of evidence at the "frontier."

These comparative outcomes show major contrasts between the roles of government as regulator and as negotiator based on scientific uncertainty. How can we interpret these findings within the literature on government bureaucracy and bargaining?

ALTERNATIVE INTERPRETATIONS: ECONOMIC AND POLITICAL INSTITUTIONALISM

This section interprets two main findings concerning the regulatory process in Europe and the United States. The first is the role of government as bureaucrat; in Europe, as a regulatory agency; in the United States, as a regulatory agency held in check by the court or legislature. The second is the role of government as a scientist. Scientific uncertainty is treated as a rationale to change regulatory decisions. In Europe, no scientists are involved, and interest groups must try to represent scientific information on their own. In the United States, scientists are involved politically, and scientific uncertainty is used by interest groups to change regulatory decisions.

Four interpretations are possible. Two are forms of economic institutionalism in which individuals, interest groups, or government bodies maximize their own benefits according to external sources like the market or institutional dominance. These include pluralism (Jasanoff 1986; Vogel 1986; Nelkin 1979; Nelkin and Pollack 1981) and the treatment of government as a competitive institution (Niskanen 1975; Weingast and Moran 1983, 1986 a and b; Moe 1984, 1987). Two other interpretations are forms of political institutionalism in which such actors develop their own interests from an internal source of identity and capacity. These include neocorporatist bargaining (Katzenstein 1985b, 1978; Hall 1986) and regulatory bargaining (Kitschelt 1989; Klapp, this volume). The following discussion analyzes the two main findings according to each of the possible interpretations.

According to pluralism, the focus is on government as a representative and nonisolated entity that regulates as well as passes and judges laws. The relations among branches of government in the United States are more pluralist in this sense than are the less representative and more isolated regulatory agencies in Europe. In the United States, concerned groups like citizens (environmentalists) and industrialists act as lobbying groups to pressure government bodies to represent their interests. Citizens use technical controversies, according to Dorothy Nelkin (1979; Nelkin and Pollack 1981), to challenge evidence, undermine analyses, and manipulate knowledge regarding risk estimates of opponents. Environmentalists or industrialists then use these vulnerabilities of regulators, Sheila Jasanoff (1986) claims, to challenge decisions or create injunctions to prevent regulators from implementing unwanted decisions. The result is that decisions in the United States are ultimately made by regulators testing their ability against legislators and judges. The U.S. court trials of Dow's use of herbicide registration despite a proposed EPA ban, and Goodrich's use of VC despite the standards of OSHA, are both rich illustrations of the politics of regulation. By contrast, the restrictive politics in Britain of the Advisory Committee on Pesticides and the intentional siting of the nuclear power plant by the British Central Electricity Governing Board show how unrepresentative and isolated the role of the regulatory agency can be in Europe.

The pluralists are also well versed in the treatment of scientific information in the United States rather than Europe. I draw from the work of David Vogel (1986); Ronald Brickman, Sheila Jasanoff, Thomas Ilgen (1985); and Joseph Badaracco (1985). Europe fosters "closed" government, where scientists generally consult only with regulators in private. Scientists are inaccessible to interest groups and seldom veer from their single interest in assisting the government. By contrast in the United States, government is "open." Scientists use controversies and uncertainties to exploit or oppose other scientists with different scientific results. These controversies may lead to change in regulatory decisions.

Scientists from Harvard and Mount Sinai debated heatedly over the presence of an active fault in the Bodega Head nuclear siting. This demonstrates the strength of scientific contest in the United States compared to Europe. In Europe, scientists were never involved in the union's "manifesto" on herbicides, nor in the Inquiry representing technical demands of citizens on the nuclear siting.

Although these pluralists deal with uncertain science, their perspective remains insufficient to understand the importance of a government agency that can remain firm. For instance, could such a perspective on pluralist and representative politics have understood why the court reinforced the position of OSHA in taking an autonomous stand on VC?

The second form of economic institutionalism focuses on the role of government bodies as competitive institutions. Here we refer to the standing debate between Niskanen (1975), Weingast and Moran (1986a), and Moe (1987). Are regulatory agencies dominant over legislatures because they can make them compete with the executive branch, like Niskanen (1975) says? This maximizes agency finances, thereby raising personal salaries and status. Or are legislatures dominant, as Weingast and Moran (1986a) say, because unless they see high standards of agency performance, they will employ strict sanctions on regulatory agencies? In the best of regulatory systems, an agency is so well-behaved regarding the interests of Congress that congresspersons almost never have to demonstrate these sanctions. If they do, oversight is the legislative tool.

These relations between bureaucrat and legislator can be imperfect, according to Moe (1987), because of the "slippage" between how bureaucrats should and do perform. This slippage is caused by competitive influences of other bodies of government like the executive and inadequate oversight resulting from a divided legislature. Probably the best illustrations of agency dominance are found in the French case in which both the National Research and Safety Institution and the National Sickness Insurance Fund were used to mesh private, public, and union interests. By contrast, the strict mode of legislative oversight is suggested in the U.S. cases. Here, the power of the court is used to both uphold OSHA in the U.S. VC case and overrule the EPA in the U.S. herbicide case.

According to this competitive institution approach, the role of scientists is relatively unimportant. None of the above authors referred to the discretion of scientific experts. I would suggest, however, that the role of scientific experts is of central importance when the "slippage" between desired action and agency performance involves issues like cancer induction. The best illustration appears to be the U.S. herbicide case in which the EPA performed a scientific analysis (Alsea II), which was discredited once the agency's own technical board (RPAR) discounted the quality of the study. The court had to consider adjusting the EPA's decision accordingly.

The other forms of institutionalism are political. The key determinants of these approaches are the internal identity and capacity of the government to have its own interests. Government is referred to as the "state" when discussed as a set of institutions with their own objectives. These institutions can compromise without losing the integrity of their organization. This means that interests do not have to be gained externally from the market or from institutional arrangements like norms, rules, or the allocation of rewards and sanctions.

State-society bargaining has been introduced by Peter Katzenstein (1978) and Steven Krasner (1978). "Society" refers to all interest groups, industrialists, and other nongovernmental actors. Two perspectives dominate: one looks at the interaction between the interests of state and private actors in making policy (Katzenstein 1984, 1985 a and b; Hall 1986; Klapp 1987 a,b,c); the other examines the resistance of private actors who avoid policies formulated by state actors (Krasner 1978; Nordlinger 1981; Skocpol 1985). Both perspectives compare economic and industrial policies across countries. Here we focus on the first perspective, toward "neocorporatism."

Neocorporatist analysis has been heralded by Keynesians as an interchange on economic and industrial policy among government bureaucrats, industrialists, and trade union leaders in advanced capitalist countries. Katzenstein (1980, 1984, 1985a) focuses his analysis on the small nations in Western Europe—particularly Austria, Switzerland, and West Germany. In these domestic economies, industrialists and politicians "neutralize" but do not undermine government efforts to make policy. They join together into a centralized core consisting of the bureaucracy, industry, labor, and political parties. These bargain informally to build consensus on industrial policies. In Austria, the dominant role of political parties in these cooperative arrangements has reduced the power of the relatively strong, centralized state to that of a hesitant entrepreneur and leader of nationalized industry. But Katzenstein finds that the same politics of consensus has led to a strengthening of the weak, decentralized state in Switzerland. The need to arbitrate between bureaucracy, unions, and international industry has forced the government into a leadership role. In both countries, corporatist relations have structured a flexible industrial policy and determined whether the state would be strong or weak (Katzenstein, 1980, 1985a, 1984).

Peter Hall (1986) clarifies that such neocorporatist bargaining actually deteriorated in Britain under Thatcher (1979–89) and in France under d'Estaing (1978–81). The Conservatives took power in Britain and staunchly repudiated the postwar Keynesian consensus of policymaking. This meant a major retreat from neocorporatist bargaining with producer groups and the trade unions. Previous governments had reduced levels of unemployment, raised social wages, and strengthened union bargaining in exchange for wage restraint by the unions. Thatcher, instead, reduced the bargaining power of the unions, reduced their capacity to strike, and rejected tripartite bargaining.

Under Giscard d'Estaing, Hall argues, France also tried to get rid of neocorporatism after 1979. But the government remained the centralized director of bargaining. This was even though only capital, not labor, and industrial development, rather than income policies, were the foci of the bargains.

Neither the British nor French cases here reflect a particularly neocorporatist analysis. The British Advisory Committee on Pesticides in charge of herbicides and the Central Electricity Generating Board siting the nuclear power reactor were *not* willing to change their decisions. Trade unions, environmentalists, local planning associations, and the Greater London Council were not sufficient opponents. In the French case, however, the government preferred not to face opposition. It used cooperative public-private government institutions to mesh public-private and union interests. These interest groups bargained for six years before they were ready for the Ministry of Labor to step in with any official regulation. Thus, the British approach resisted bargaining, while the French approach used cooperation to undermine the eventual need for regulation.

The neocorporatist approach also does not explicitly address the role of scientists in policymaking. The cases are not analyzing scientific issues. Hall treats the issue of monetarists versus Keynesians only to show how technical experts could equally support either corporatist or noncorporatist policies.

The fourth interpretation represents this state-society bargaining approach, but focuses on these two changes in theorizing about the state. I argue that one change is to study the role of the state as a scientist in environmental and public health contexts. This is a new dimension in that scientific information and uncertainty are used explicitly for political gain. I believe that this is an innovation within a state-centered framework, although it has been raised earlier in the discussion of the science of knowledge. The second change is the role of the state as a regulator. This may be less innovative theoretically since Katzenstein (1985a, 1978) Hall (1986), and others have already studied the state as an economic and industrial actor. Herbert Kitschelt (1989) and I seek only to shift the focus to the state as a regulator.

In the first change, science plays a powerful role to gain political advantage. The role of scientific uncertainty, in particular, is critical because, different from certain information, it can be used as a pivotal bargaining resource or rationale. Interest groups use uncertainties as political resources to bolster their own demands that regulatory agencies change decisions. Legislators and judges, however, are dominant over agencies and use uncertainties as rationales to retain or change decisions. These supervisory bodies use the uncertainties strategically to adjust who is responsible and by how much, regarding the proof of carcinogenicity and safety of substances.

The key factor is whether scientists are willing to supply interest groups with these pivotal uncertainties, or are only willing to supply them to government authorities behind closed doors. The cases show that scientists are politically active in the United States but not in Europe. The result is that in the three European cases discussed here, the agencies use their own scientific analyses however performed. By contrast, in the United States cases regulatory agencies run into conflicts of interest with legislators or judges. Scientific analyses become open and politicized as a result of these conflicts.

The cases show, therefore, that the state as scientist can push its *own* institutional interpretation of the scientific evidence in Europe. In both the British herbicide and nuclear power cases, as well as in the more cooperative French VC case, regulatory agencies used scientists to act as scientific judges. Scientists and regulators were motivated by their own internal institutional interests to judge how science should be applied, and to regulate accordingly—*not* by domineering or subverting opponents. The interpretation of science, therefore, is a direct function of the scientific aims and regulatory independence of the state to govern.

In the United States, by contrast, the cases demonstrate a predominant capacity of supervisory courts or legislature to rule. Both these courts and legislature represent the elected interests of the state. This is even true for the court, because an elected official appoints judges. These electoral interests represent the concerns of public interest groups. This means that in the cases, the courts or legislature intended to supervise the introduction of science by regulatory agencies. This was true whether the courts or legislature supported the regulatory agency's scientific analysis—upholding the VC regulations—or reversed the agency's scientific analysis—striking down the ban on registration of herbicides.

Supervisory bodies thus play "pluralistic" roles in judging the science of regulatory agencies. If the bodies agree with the scientific interpretation of the agency, they give it added power. But when they disagree, they challenge and even strike down the agency's scientific interpretation. This is where the regulatory agency's own state-centered determination of scientific validity will not be upset by supervisory pluralism as long as some resolution of scientific truth occurs.

The second change, regulatory bargaining, examines the role of the state in several technological, public health, and environmental situations. Herbert Kitschelt (1989) looks at technology policy in Europe, the United States, and Japan. My earlier book (Klapp 1987c) examines the shift from a regulatory to an entrepreneurial policy in guiding oil industrialization in advanced and less-developed capitalist countries. The present book, by contrast, looks at the regulation of public health, technological safety, and environmental quality in the United States, Britain, and France.

As a regulator, the state is both relatively weak and relatively strong compared to the economic and industrial policy studied by Katzenstein (1978, 1984, 1985a) Krasner (1978), Skocpol (1985), and Klapp (1987c). It is relatively weak in that the regulatory state, different from state enterprise, for instance, cannot guide private and state investments, bank loans and subsidies, or sectoral development. Instead, it can only help support state involvement by bailing out dying companies, subsidizing weak industries, or providing regulations to protect citizens from health or environmental harm. But the state as regulator can also be relatively strong. It can tax, license, limit production, and restrict production for health and environmental protection.

Regulatory state and society relations are quite different in Europe than they are in the United States. In Britain and France, bureaucratic branches (regulatory agencies) remain autonomous in regulating herbicides, VC, and nuclear power plant sites. They perform a centralized role, which is *not* checked by other branches of the government. Nor have relations between the government and citizens appeared to be important. In fact, in the European cases analyzed here, information was exchanged behind "closed doors" so that it could remain private between government officials and scientists. Scientific uncertainty *never* was used as a public resource in the cases. When it did enter the view of citizens or workers (in the British nuclear and French VC cases), it was organized legally or institutionally so that any uncertainty in the science could not prevail.

By contrast, the relations between regulatory state and society are pluralistic in the United States. Regulatory bargains were reversed for saccharin, herbicides, and nuclear power plant sites, and reinforced for dioxin, VC, and LNG. These bargains are often the result of courts or legislatures acting as outside options on behalf of citizens, industrialists, workers, or even scientists. Scientific uncertainty is used strategically as a resource for these interest groups, and as a rationale for the supervisory outside options in government (court or legislature). The bargains that result are pluralistic in the number of interest groups and the different government bodies involved. Sometimes these bargains require the regulatory agency to withdraw from regulation, as in the saccharin case. Other times, the court reinforces the agency's use of science at its "frontier," as in the VC case.

Whether as scientist or regulator, the U.S. state is more pluralist, while the European state is more centralized. If a citizen, scientist, industrialist, or worker wants the option to challenge regulatory decisions in the courts or through the legislature, then perhaps the U.S. state offers the best opportunity. But if those diverse interests could work together within a cooperative bureaucratic institution, as in France, then perhaps public health, technological safety, and environmental quality could progress using an inspired but centralized state regulator.

APPENDIX: NATIONAL CASE STUDIES IN EUROPE AND THE UNITED STATES

British Opposition to Licensing of Herbicide 2,4,5-T

In regulating the herbicide 2,4,5-T, the British government again rebuked scientific pleas, this time from agricultural workers. This occurred despite other herbicide bans: 1973 in Norway, 1977 in Sweden, and 1979 in the United States. The British Parliament questioned whether 2,4,5-T should be regulated in the United Kingdom.

The herbicide 2,4,5-T is used to control broad-leafed brush and weeds in agricultural areas, forests, and along rights of way. It decomposes quickly in soil or water, and does not affect the quality of the groundwater or air. The manufacture of the herbicide, however, does not chemically synthesize the most toxic chlorodibenzodioxin know, 2,3,7,8-TCDD (tetrachlorodibenzo-P-dioxin). This chemical is suspected to cause carcinogenic and mutagenic effects and fetal abnormalties (Brickman et al. 1985: 212).

In 1979 the Advisory Committee on Pesticides examined the question of 2,4,5-T use for agricultural purposes. This agency reports directly to the Ministry of Agriculture, Fisheries, and Food on the safety and use of pesticides. The ACP stated that no epidemiological evidence or animal tests showed that the herbicide endangered the health of agricultural workers (Brickman et al. 1985: 203).

Concerned about their exposure to 2,4,5-T, workers in the National Union of Agricultural and Allied Workers published a manifesto, "The 2,4,5-T Dossier—Not One Minute Longer" in March 1980. This publication indicated that workers and their families had suffered from sickness and miscarriages. Workers claimed that existing animal experiments and epidemiological studies were insufficient to present their case based on scientifically collected and analyzed data. Although Brickman et al. (1985) claim that this "Dossier" was "intended to raise the emotional pitch of the debate," workers were clearly constrained by this lack of certified scientific evidence (Brickman et al. 1985: 214; ERL 1986).

The definition of scientific "proof" was also ambiguous and hotly contested. NUAWW insisted that all chemicals should be proven through scientific study and experimentation not to cause adverse effects in animals or people. Their focus was on "safety." They argued that the ACP should identify a "balance of probabilities" that would be "unsafe" as long as damage to health was the most probable. But the government's ACP stood firm that unless evidence showed a strong positive correlation between human contact with the herbicide and adverse health impacts, there was no reason to ban the substance. This reflected MAFF's concern about "danger" instead of "safety." This perspective represented the "beyond all reasonable doubt" view of proof which is used in criminal law and by scientists (ERL 1986: R-6).

During 1979–80 NUAWW made great efforts to get the ACP to ban 2,4,5-T. When it did not succeed, the union instead convinced several large industrial consumers of the herbicide to discontinue their uses. NUAWW also compelled the control organization of trade unions, the Trade Unions Congress, to call for a ban (Brickman et al. 1985: 214)

Despite this overwhelming support for NUAWW, the ACP refused to ban 2,4,5-T. In 1980 and 1982 ACP published detailed reports on the herbicide, which emphasized the nonpositive epidemiological evidence. They also criticized the Alsea II study performed in the United States. Alsea II was an epidemiological analysis of six years of data showing a strong correlation between herbicide spraying in the Alsea basin in Oregon and the local miscarriage rate. Instead, the ACP stated that virtually no human risk existed at very low levels of worker exposure. After the disclosure, however, the ACP did agree to a code of practice to control the use of 2,4,5-T. But the ACP stressed that it would make recommendations only on medical and scientific grounds. It would not, the ACP emphasized, submit to political expediency as had other countries like Germany (ERL 1986: R-8, 11; Brickman et al. 1985: 213–214).

The British regulatory agency for pesticides therefore refused to concede to worker's demands for a ban of 2,4,5-T. Despite increasing opposition due to scientific uncertainty, regulatory agencies refused to bargain with workers, environmentalists, or industrialists. Different from the reliance of U.S. interest groups on the courts or legislature, these outside options were not explored by British workers or environmentalists. The institutional constraints on making a legal claim in Britain remained exceedingly difficult. The next case, moreover, shows that concerned groups also did not gain major concessions in the siting of a nuclear power plant.

British Opposition to the Siting of the Sizewell B Nuclear Power Plant

The government in Britain was no less stalwart in quelling challenges from environmentalists opposed to a new nuclear power plant. Part of its success, however, was the government's claim that only scientific challenges would be considered. Political demands or public anxieties were simply not reviewed. In 1979 the Conservative government announced the need for a new type of pressurized water reactor (of the type that had failed at Three Mile Island in the United States). A Public Inquiry was scheduled in 1982 to look into the proposed siting for the PWR at Sizewell in Suffolk County. Whereas most inquiries took several months, the Sizewell B Inquiry lasted from 1983 to 1987, and involved 195 witnesses, 4,330 supporting documents, and about the same number of letters of objections.

According to the standards prescribed by the Nuclear Installations Inspectorate (NII), the total frequency of all incidents leading to uncontrollable releases of radioactivity had to be less than 10^{-6} per reactor per year (O'Riordan 1987: 204). But for Sizewell B, this frequency was to be less than 1×10^{-7} per year (British Department of Energy 1986).

The design engineers of the government's Central Electricity Generating Board tried to deflect any challenges to their proposal. They had produced both event- and fault-tree analyses for about 12 categories of potential technical problems, including inadvertent closures of mainstream isolation valves, loss of electricity, or loss of the main cooling water supply (O'Riordan 1987: 205–206).

But several shortcomings of their probabilistic risk analyses were identified by experts of Friends of the Earth (FOE), who strongly objected to the reactor (Richard Davies interview, 2/27/88). One key issue was whether the CEGB could realistically claim that the Sizewell B would meet the above NII criterion of 10^{-6} radioactive releases per reactor per year. This was especially doubtful considering the probabilities of common-mode failures when the same technological parts serve more than one function. CEGB engineers insisted that estimates of probability were biased in the conservative direction to accommodate inevitable statistical uncertainties. But even the head of the Safety and Reliability Directorate of the UK Atomic Energy Authority admitted that many other important hazards and systemic uncertainties in plant operation had been avoided by such a narrow focus on only statistical uncertainty.

The major opposition to the plant's safety, however, came from FOE, the Town and Country Planning Association, and the Greater London Council (disbanded in 1986). About 4,000 letters objecting to the plant's construction were sent to the inspector of the Inquiry. The overwhelming political concern was that the industry was involved in a collusion with the government to promote nuclear power in Britain despite its problems. Accidents at Windscale in Britain, Three Mile Island in the United States, and Chernobyl in the Soviet Union were fresh in the minds of opponents. These accidents raised public anxieties about uncertainty, the unknown, and the unknowable. Citizens were also concerned about British civil servants who might discount the possibility of accidents because they did not have technical training (Davies 1987: 103–107; O'Riordan 1987: 215).

The Inquiry decided not to recognize these anxieties about the safety of nuclear power unless they were stated as scientific claims. This was a brilliant tactical strategy to ignore opposition. As a result, the CEGB and other proponents of nuclear power eventually won the struggle to construct the Sizewell B nuclear power plant. The government approved the project in March 1987. This outcome, however, was a mixed blessing. The government went ahead without the backing of many people directly affected.

The uncertainties of nuclear power incited no less opposition from environmentalists than had uncertainties of herbicides aroused trade union groups also in Britain. Both environmentalists and trade unions fell short by not seeking the assistance of the courts. As a result, in both cases regulatory agencies remained firm in their initial decisions. They compelled environmentalists and industrialists to comply. A similar story of unified governmental authority took place in France regarding vinyl chloride regulation. This unified authority, however, was based on explicit cooperation with potential opponents: industrialists and trade unions.

Lack of French Opposition to a Standard for Exposure to Vinyl Chloride

The vinyl chloride industry was structured to take advantage of industrial cooperation regarding occupational health controls in France. This resulted from the collective efforts of industry, trade unions, and government to reduce exposure levels for workers. As in the United States, the concentrations of VC in French factories were extremely high between the late 1940s and the 1960s—between 300 and 1,000 ppm. In 1974, however, the B.F. Goodrich company announced that some workers in a VC plant had died from angiosarcoma of the liver. This was a great shock to the populace (case draws from Badaracco 1985: 82–93).

In 1974, the Association of Procedures of Plastic Materials immediately formed an ad hoc committee to deal with the issue of VC's cancer-causing potential. The Association represented the interests of producers of VC and polyvinyl chloride (PVC). Medical data, measurement techniques for recording VC levels, and methods of controlling exposure to VC were studied. All information was shared among producers. Furthermore, an extensive epidemiological review of worker health histories and medical records was initiated to find cases of cancer, particularly angiosarcoma of the liver. Workers were kept well informed of both the information being collected and the health hazards due to VC. To expedite exposure reduction, producers began to plug leaks and to install VC monitoring technologies (Badaracco 1985: 85).

At the same time, the National Research and Safety Institute (l'Institut National de Recherche et de Sécurité, INRS), moved toward creating regulations for VC exposure levels in factories. The INRS is a "quango" administered equally by the government, producers, and labor unions. In 1975 and 1976 it recommended a reduction in exposure levels at first to daily average of 10 ppm and not exceeding 25 ppm. The next year daily averages were 5 ppm with a ceiling at 15 ppm. In 1976 another quango intervened, the National Sickness Insurance Fund (Caisse Nationale de l'Assurance Maladie, CN) which is responsible for worker safety and compensation. It issued a notice in 1976 distinguishing between acceptable exposure levels of 5–15 ppm at older plants and stricter levels of 1–5 ppm at new factories. The CN also stressed the importance of reducing VC concentrations to zero because of the impossibility of establishing a safe exposure level for carcinogens. This

was a very conservative position to take. Although these recommendations were not legally binding, the cooperation between government,
producers, and labor unions helped to reduce VC levels greatly within
only two years (Badaracco 1985: 85–87). This effectiveness of quangos
in France contrasts starkly with their devalued worth in England as
publicly chartered advisory bodies (Richard Lester, personal communication, 8/22/88).

The dearth of controversy in France over scientific data and risk
analyses was surprising. Equally curious was the short-lived opposition
to VC reduction efforts by the Confédération Générale du Travail, a
communist union. Initially the CGT complained that workers were being
used as guinea pigs and that VC represented the classic confrontation
between workers and capitalists. They demanded an exposure limit of 1
ppm like OSHA had required in the United States. These charges soon
ceased, however, as the CGT recognized that it shared common objectives with producers in reducing VC exposure levels, even if it disagreed
on the ultimate levels achievable (Badaracco 1985: 88–89).

The government's Ministry of Labor entered late in the game. In 1980
it issued a legally binding decree on VC standards. Although the six-year
period prior to this official regulation seems long, it served several
purposes. The Ministry wanted producers to feel that sufficient thought,
analysis, and trials by industry underlay eventual regulations. Because
violators were subject to fines and even imprisonment, clarity about the
scientific evidence and about the nature of "reasonable" decisions were
preconditions for regulations. The proposed limits on VC were also
evaluated first by an advisory council composed of producers and labor
representatives. No one was therefore surprised when the regulations
were finally published in 1980. The Ministry of Labor required a weekly
average exposure level of 1 ppm with not more than 5 ppm in future
plants and a weekly average of 3 ppm in existing factories. It also required
that records of exposure levels be available to workers, the CN, and
Ministry inspectors. The six years of precompliance by producers
explains why no legal suit was brought against the Ministry after the
regulations were published.

This case of French cooperation among regulatory agencies, industrialists, and trade unions appears to be unique approach to the authority
of government control. By contrast, the cases of herbicides, nuclear
power, and VC in the United States show the consequences of suscepti-
bility to scientific uncertainties or to court challenges.

American Opposition to Licensing of Herbicide 2,4,5-T

The herbicide 2,4,5-T was one of the earliest agrochemicals regulated by the EPA (direct summary from Brickman et al. 1985: 212–213). The EPA decided to halt all uses of the chemical on food crops when the president's scientific advisor indicated that laboratory tests on animals showed birth defects in offspring. But the agency was eventually slowed in its regulatory proceedings by its complete lack of quantitative data to defend its claim about this association between use and health effects. This lack was quickly filled when the EPA carried out the Alsea II study. This showed a strong epidemiological correlation between the rate of miscarriages over a six-year period and the use of the herbicide to spray Oregon's Alsea basin. Based on the study, the EPA immediately suspended the registration of 2,4,5-T for use on forests and rights of way. Dow Chemical Company took the agency to court to defend its regulation.

The EPA's own RPAR process continued to review other uses of the herbicide. But the Scientific Advisory Board found that the available data including the Alsea II study did not provide evidence that the herbicide was an immediate or substantial threat to human health or the environment. The panel recommended against cancellation of the registration of the herbicide's use on rice and range lands. Soon after, the agency and the manufacturers of 2,4,5-T began to negotiate an out-of-court settlement. But in 1983 Dow requested that EPA cancel all of its registrations of the herbicide. Dow argued that its profits from the chemical were not offsetting the legal and administrative costs necessary to defend it (Brickman et al 1985: 212–213).

The case demonstrates how differently regulation occurred in the United States versus Europe. In the United States, the court began to reverse the regulatory agency based on improved scientific knowledge. By contrast, in Europe the regulatory agency stood firm. The siting of nuclear power was analogous in its scientific conviction.

American Opposition to the Siting of a Nuclear Power Plant at Bodega Head, California

Environmentalists objected to uncertainties that were discovered about the safety of the site. This was similar to the opposition in the British nuclear case. But in the U.S. case, environmentalists also disparaged nuclear power on purely political grounds.

By 1963 the Pacific Gas and Electric Company presented the AEC with a proposal to site a nuclear reactor at Bodega Head, just north of San Francisco, California. The proposal was for a conventional steam-electric generating plant but with a 300,000 kilowatt capacity, larger than any built (case draws on Meehan [1984]). PGE had already gained the approval of the county and the state Public Utilities Commission. All that the electric company needed now was AEC approval for the reactor and site (Meehan 1984: 5-6).

The key issues was whether the site was safe for a nuclear reactor. Preliminary geological studies by a PGE consultant had indicated that the site was distant from centers of population and located on a solid granite foundation of bedrock. It was not clear, however, whether the site was threatened by or was associated with faulting of bedrock. The site was just west of the San Andreas fault, a major seam in the earth's crust running the full length of California and separating the Pacific "plate" from the continental "plate" the United States Periodic shifting of this fault cases branch faulting in subsidiary "zones of apparent weakness" (Meehan 1984: 5).

Initial risk assessments by the AEC indicated that the reactor plant would meet the agency's risk guidelines. The frequency of all incidents triggered by a fault and leading to a release of radiation should be less than one in a hundred million (1×10^{-8}) per reactor per year. Bodega was designed to meet this criterion. The AEC guidelines also indicated that ground rupture beneath a power plant could be up to three feet of horizontal movement. The probability of this occurring could only be one in a hundred thousand (10^{-5}) per year. The USGS and AEC estimated that a maximum displacement of this sort would be no more than three feet at Bodega Head, and that the probability of this occurring was exactly that set by the ACRS. The reactor plant also met the proposed guidelines of the AEC that annual risks of physical harm due to some radioactive release should be less than one in a million chances for the general population (Meehan 1984: 133).

But a major controversy among scientist and engineers occurred over the chances of a fault at or near the site. The USGS had contradictory reports. One report noted that although the quartz-diorite bedrock was fractured into a sugary consistency, the sand cap above it had not been disturbed by previous earthquakes over thousands of years. Another seismology report examined the tremors and strong shaking that might occur due to earthquakes near the site, a factor left out of the first report. This report concluded that in a worst-case scenario the reactor might *not* survive an earthquake (Meehan 1984: 11-13).

To make matters worse, David Pesonen, a Berkeley activist, launched a scientific attack on the PGE proposal. With the aid of a consultant geologist, he claimed that the site was completely unsuitable for a nuclear reactor (Meehan 1984: 8).

To the surprise of all, an active fault was found in the terrace sand and gravel straight down to the bedrock and running across the proposed site for the reactor. The USGS geologists estimated that it could move 2–11 feet in the future (Meehan 1984: 13–16). Simultaneous with this scientific controversy, a confrontation was emerging between PGE and the Sierra Club together with Pesonen.

By 1964 the AEC terminated the reactor proposal for Bodega Head on its own! The AEC report concluded that "enough uncertainties" existed at the Bodega site for the proposed plant to prevent it from being used (Meehan 1984).

Different from the British case, irrefutable scientific uncertainty forced the AEC to concede to opposition groups. The evidence was an active fault discovered at the site. But the agency also implicitly responded to the political opposition posed by environmentalists and other protest groups. This political assessment differs from the British nuclear case in which the Public Inquiry simply refused to consider nonscientific claims. The final case of VC regulation in the United States also demonstrates the power of the courts and of scientific evidence.

American Opposition to a Standard for Exposure to Vinyl Chloride

The creation of a standard limiting the exposure of workers to concentrations of vinyl chloride in the United States is a classic case of adversarial science pitting a regulatory agency against industry (Badaracco 1985). Vinyl chloride is a chemical that has been used over the past 30 years to manufacture phonograph records, upholstery, plastic wrap, and numerous other consumer products. Imperceptible leaks in containment vessels and contact during routine practices of maintaining systems are the main sources of exposure for workers. Average exposure levels were as high as 500 ppm in the early 1970s. A shock came in 1973 when studies at the Institute for Oncology in Bologna, Italy, showed that VC appeared to cause tumors in rats exposed to concentrations of 500 ppm and 250 ppm. But the real blow came when B.F. Goodrich, a major manufacturer of VC in the United States, announced in 1974 that three workers from its Louisville PVC plant had died from cancer-related angiosarcoma of the liver. These deaths were directly linked to exposure to VC and gas. The threat of an epidemic loomed as the death toll rose to 19 workers over the next few months (Badaracco 1985: 10–11, 42).

The Occupational Safety and Health Administration immediately announced a rule-making procedure consisting of a Notice of Proposed Regulation followed by a Hearing for Public Comment. But public fear pressured OSHA into implementing an Emergency Temporary Standard that workers not be exposed to levels exceeding 50 ppm. No studies had shown that VC unquestionably induced cancer at that level and it seemed the lowest concentration achievable by industry at the time. OSHA's choice of 50 ppm gained credibility when the Manufacturing Chemists Association released findings of angiosarcoma of the liver in rats exposed to that dose of VC. In May 1974 the agency published its Proposed Standard of 1 ppm. Along with this proposal, OSHA announced that public hearings would be held in which industry, labor, and the public could voice concerns. By October 1974 the agency had already set a final standard of an average of 1 ppm and a ceiling of 5 ppm (Badaracco 1985: 42–44, 53). OSHA was constrained by its statute to adopt a standard that "assumes . . . that no employee will suffer material impairment of health" (Badaracco 1985: 49).

Industry was furious. The second study by the Manufacturing Chemists Association was an epidemiological review that found a statistically significant rise did *not* occur in the number of liver cancer victims among vinyl chloride workers compared to U.S. males in general. Moreover, industry studies of employee health records showed that angiosarcomas of the liver were present only in older workers who had been exposed to extremely high levels of VC during the early 1960s (Badaracco 1985: 44).

The workers countered with medical evidence on their side. Officials of the AFL-CIO claimed that VC was a human carcinogen so that no level of exposure was safe. This claim was supported by a study of the Mount Sinai School of Medicine, which reported lung infections in 58 percent of Goodyear workers and brain and lymphatic cancer in those involved in VC production. The Harvard School of Public Health also issued a study of 161 records of deceased VC and PVC workers, which indicated 50 percent more deaths had occurred due to brain and liver cancers. Finally, the National Cancer Institute determined that there was no threshold of exposure to carcinogens below which it was "safe" (Badaracco 1985: 43–44, 50).

These disparate epidemiological findings stirred the political battle to new intensity. The Society of the Plastics Industry representing B.F. Goodrich, Shell Chemical, and Dow Chemical was irate. It had from the start engaged in industrywide sharing of information, reviews of medical records, and purchasing of monitoring equipment. SPI resented OSHA's radical stance and argued that only a moderate and phased decrease in exposure levels was technologically and economically viable. It recommended an average exposure level of 10 ppm by 1976. When OSHA announced its final standard of 1 ppm, SPI and six companies sued the agency in the Second Circuit Court of Appeals in New York (The Society of the Plastics Industry v. OSHA [Badaracco 1985: 42–48]).

Labor unions including the United Rubber Workers, the Oil, Chemical and Atomic Workers, and the AFL-CIO intervened on behalf of OSHA. The AFL-CIO also wrote letters to OSHA officials, President Nixon and senators. These letters lauded OSHA's action and claimed that VC was destroying the work force in "epidemic proportions" (Badaracco 1985: 44, 47).

The courts decided to uphold OSHA's standard. The Second Circuit Court of New York recognized that the VC hazard was on the "frontiers of scientific knowledge." The court also stated, however, that OSHA had the duty to defend the health of workers even when research and risk assessment was "deficient." The Supreme Court of New York refused to hear the case on appeal (Badaracco 1985: 53–54).

Surprisingly, OSHA tests indicated that 90 percent of the industry was already conforming to the 1 ppm standard by 1976 (Badaracco 1985: 55). Thus, compliance had been achieved. The price, however, had been a tremendously controversial and combative bargaining process. In the end, the courts had upheld the regulatory authority of OSHA. Uncertainties about vinyl chloride still remained politically charged.

Bibliography

Abraham, Kenneth and Richard Merrill. "Scientific Uncertainty in the Courts." *Issues in Science and Technology*, Winter 1986.

Allison, Graham. *The Essence of Decision* (Boston: Little, Brown, 1971).

Armstrong, B. and R. Doll. "Bladder Cancer Mortality in Diabetics in Relation to Saccharine Consumption and Smoking Habits." *British Journal of Preventive Medicine*, Vol. 29, 1975.

Armstrong, B., A. Lea, A. Adelstein, J. Donovan, G. White, and S. Ruttle. "Cancer Mortality and Saccharin Consumption in Diabetics." *British Journal of Preventive Social Medicine*, Vol. 29, 1976.

Bacharach, Samuel and Edward Lawler. *Bargaining: Power, Tactics, and Outcomes* (San Francisco: Jossey-Bass, 1981).

Badaracco, Joseph, Jr. *Loading the Dice* (Boston: Harvard Business School Press, 1985).

Barnes, Barry and David Edge (eds.). *Science in Context: Readings in the Sociology of Science* (Cambridge, Mass.: MIT Press, 1982).

Bazelon, David. "Science and Uncertainty: A Jurist's View." *Harvard Environmental Law Review*, Vol. 209, 1981.

Beer, Samuel, Suzanne Berger, Guido Goldmand, and Adam Ulam. *Patterns of Government: The Major Political Systems of Europe*, 3rd ed. (New York: Random House, 1972).

Bell, Daniel. "The Measurement of Knowledge and Technology." In Eleanor Sheldon and Wilbert Moore (eds.), *Indicators of Social Change, Concepts and Measurements* (New York: Russell Sage, 1968).

Benveniste, Guy. *The Politics of Expertise* (Berkeley: Glendessary Press, 1972).

Berry, Brian. *Political Argument* (London: Routledge and Kegan Paul, 1965).

Brickman, Ronald, Sheila Jasanoff, and Thomas Ilgen. *Controlling Chemicals* (Ithaca, NY: Cornell University Press, 1985).

British Department of Energy. "Sizewell B Public Inquiry," report by Sir Frank Layfield. Vol. I, Part I, presented December 5, 1986 (London: HMSO, 1986).

Brooks, Harvey. "The Resolution of Technically Intensive Public Policy Disputes." *Science, Technology and Human Values*, Vol. 9, No. 1, Winter 1984.

Brooks, Harvey and Chester L. Cooper (eds.). *Science for Public Policy* (Elmsford, N.Y.: Pergamon Press, 1987).

Burns, John, Vice-President, Hoffman-La Roche, Inc. Testimony offered to Subcommittee on Health and Scientific Research, Committee on Human Resources, U.S. Senate, 95th Congress, hearing on *The Banning of Saccharine, 1977*, June 7, 1977 (Washington, D.C.: U.S. Government Printing Office, 1977), p. 60.

Buser, H. R. and H. P. Bosshardt. *Mitt. Gebiete Lebenson Hyg.* 69, 191 (1978) in J.W.A., Lustenhower, K. Olie, and O. Hutzinger, "Chlorinated Dibenzo-p-Dioxins and Related Compounds in Incinerator Effluents: A Review of Measurements and Mechanisms of Formation," *Chemosphere*, vol. 9 1980: 501–522.

Canadian National Health and Welfare Ministry (CNHWM). Health Protection Branch. *Canadian Position on Saccharin.* Ottawa: CNHWM, March 7, 1977.

Capuzzo, Judith. "PCBs in Buzzards Bay, MA: Effects on Energetics and Reproductive Cycles of Bivalve Molluscs." Sea Grant Project R/p-20, July 1984–June 1986.

Capuzzo, Judith, John Teal, and Robert Bastian. "Ecological and Human Health Criteria for Cross Ecosystem Comparison of Impacts of Waste Management Practice." Unpublished paper, WHOI Contribution 5925. Woods Hole Oceanographic Institution, 1984.

Chamberlain, N. W. *Collective Bargaining* (New York: McGraw-Hill, 1951).

Chatterjee, Kalyan "Disagreement in Bargaining: Models With Incomplete Information." In Alvin Roth (ed.), *Game-Theoretic Models of Bargaining* (Cambridge: Cambridge University Press, 1985).

Coase, Ronald. "The Nature of the Firm," *Economica*, Vol. 4, November 1937, pp. 386–405.

Commoner, Barry et al. "Activities of the Municipal Solid Waste Community Information Service." Queens College, New York, January 1984–July 1985.

Commoner, Barry, Michael McNamara, Karen Shapiro, and Thomas Webster. *Environmental and Economic Analysis of Alternative Municipal Solid Waste Disposal Technologies*, Vols. I–III (Vol. I published May 1, 1984; revised August, 1984) Center for the Biology of Natural Systems, Queens College, New York, December 1, 1984.

Conrad, J. (ed.) *Society, Technology and Risk Assessment* (London: Academic Press, 1980).

Covello, Vincent, Lester Lave, Alan Moghissi, and V.R.R. Uppuluri (eds.). *Uncertainty in Risk Assessment, Risk Management, and Decision Making* (New York: Plenum Press, 1984).

Crouch, Edmund and Richard Wilson. *Risk/Benefit Analysis* (Cambridge, Mass: Ballinger, 1982).

Crozier, Michael. *The Bureaucratic Phenomenon* (Chicago: University of Chicago Press, 1964).

Davies, Richard. "The Effectiveness of the Sizewell B Public Inquiry in Facilitating Communication about the Risks of Nuclear Power." *Science, Technology and Human Values*, Vol. 12, Issues 3 and 4, Summer/Fall 1987, pp. 102–110.

_____. "The Sizewell B Nuclear Inquiry: An Analysis of Public Participation in Decisionmaking about Nuclear Power." *Science, Technology and Human Values*, Vol. 9, Issue 3, Summer 1984.

Department of Sanitation (DOS), City of New York. *Draft Environmental Impact Statement for The Proposed Resource Recovery Facility at the Brooklyn Navy Yard* (DEIS). September 1984.

_____. *Final Environmental Impact Statement Proposed Resource Recovery Facility at the Brooklyn Navy Yard* (FEIS), Appendix D: Technical Appendix Vol. III, prepared by Camp Dresser and McKee, June 1985.

Deutsch, Karl. *The Analysis of International Relations* (Englewood Cliffs, N.J.: Prentice-Hall, 1968).

Douglas, Mary and Aaron Wildavsky. *Risk and Culture* (Berkeley: University of California Press, 1982).

Efron, Edith. *The Apocalyptics* (New York: Simon and Schuster, 1984).

Ellul, Jacques. *The Technological Society* (New York: Alfred Knopf, 1965).

Environmental Protection Agency (EPA). *Risk Assessment and Management: Framework for Decision Making* EPA 600/9-85-002, December 1984a.

_____. Office of Pesticides and Toxic Substances. "Assessments of Emissions of Specific Compounds from a Resource Recovery Municipal Refuse Incinerator." Final Report, June 1984b (EPA-560/5-84-002).

EPA, Office of Public Affairs. *Environmental News*, August 14, 1986.

Environmental Resources Limited (ERL). *Uncertainty in Environmental Decision Making* (London: Environmental Resources Ltd., 1986).

Etzioni, Amitai and Sam Nun. "The Public Appreciation of Science in Contemporary America." *Daedalus*, Vol. 103, No. 3, 1974.

Evans, Peter, Dietrich Rueschemeyer, and Theda Skocpol (eds.). "On the Road Towards a More Adequate Understanding of the State." In *Bringing the State Back In* (Cambridge: Cambridge University Press, 1985).

Fairley, William B. "Comments for the Federal Power Commission Draft Environmental Impact Statement for the Construction and Operation of an LNG Import Terminal at Everett, Massachusetts." February 1976, published in Federal Power Commission Final Environmental Impact Statement, September 1976.

Fay, James. "Comments on Draft Environmental Impact Statement for the Construction and Operation of an LNG Import Terminal at Everett, Mass." Docket Nos. CP 73-135, CP 73-137, CP 74-227, and CP 76-9, Federal Power Commission, Bureau of Natural Gas, published in Final Environmental Impact Statement, September 1976.

_____. "Risks of LNG and LPG." *Annual Review of Energy 1980*, Annual Reviews, Inc., 1980.

_____. "Experimental Observations of Entrainment Rates in Dense Gas Dispersion Tests." In G. Ooms and H. Tennekes (eds.), *Atmospheric Dispersion of Heavy Gases and Small Particles* (New York: Springer-Verlag, 1984).

Fay, James and David Lewis, Jr. "The Inflammability and Dispersion of LNG Vapor Clouds." Paper presented at Fourth International Symposium on Transport of Hazardous Cargoes by Sea and Inland Waterways, Jacksonville, Florida, October 26–30, 1975.

Fay James and Stephen Zemba. "Dispersion of Initially Compact Dense Gas Clouds." *Atmospheric Environment*, Vol. 19, No. 8, 1985.

_____. "A Conservative Method for Estimating Gas Concentrations in Dense Gas Plumes." Department of Mechanical Engineering, MIT, 86-42.2, 1986.

Federal Power Commission (FPC), Bureau of Natural Gas. *Final Environmental Impact Statement for the Construction and Operation of an LNG Import Terminal at Everett, Massachusetts (Port of Boston)*, September 1976.

Feldman, Elliot and Jerome Milch. *Technocracy Versus Democracy: The Comparative Politics of International Airports* (Boston: Auburn House, 1982).

Ferreira, Joseph and Stephen Hill. "Mechanisms for Sharing the Costs of Large Accidents." Energy Impacts Project, Laboratory of Architecture and Planning, March 1979.

Fischhoff, Baruch. "Managing Risk Perception." *Issues in Science and Technology*, Vol. II, No. I, Fall 1985.

Fisher, Roger. "Negotiating Power." *Behavioral Science*, Vol. 27, 1983.

Fisher, Roger and William Ury. *Getting to Yes* (Boston: Houghton Mifflin, 1981).

Food and Administration (FDA). Food, Drug, and Cosmetics Act of 1958. FDA proposed ban on saccharin according to Section 348 of Food Additives Amendment of 1958 (the Delaney Clause). U.S. Congress repealed proposed ban in November 1977 (the Saccharin Study and Labeling Act of 1977).

Fudenberg, D. and J. Tirole. "Sequential Bargaining with Incomplete Information." *Review of Economic Studies*, Vol. 50, 1983.

Gardensford, Peter and Nils-Eric Sahlin. "Unreliable Probabilities, Risk-Taking, and Decision Making." *Sunthese*, Vol. 53, 1982, pp. 361–386.

Gillespie, Brendan, Dave Eva, and Roy Johnston. "Carcinogenic Risk Assessment in the United States and Great Britain: The Case of Aldrin/Dieldrin." *Social Studies of Science* (London), Vol. 9, 1979.

Graham, John, Laura Green, and Marc Roberts. *Seeking Safety: Science, Public Policy, and Cancer Risk* (Cambridge, Mass.: Harvard University Press, 1989).

Haimes, Yacov. "Risk-Benefit Analysis in a Multiobjective Framework." In Yacov Haimes (ed.), *Risk-Benefit Analysis in Water Resources Planning and Management* (New York: Plenum Press, 1981).

Hall, Peter. *Governing the Economy: The Politics of State Intervention in Britain and France* (Cambridge: Polity Press, 1986).

Hallenbeck, William. *Quantitative Risk Assessment for Environmental and Occupational Health* (Chelsea, Mich.: Lewis Publishers, 1986).

Hammond, Kenneth, Barry Anderson, Jeffrey Sutherland, and Barbara Marvin. "Improving Scientists' Judgements of Risk." *Risk Analysis*, Vol. 4, No. 1, 1984.

Hart, Fred C. and Associates, Inc. "Assessment of Potential Public Health Impacts Associated with Predicted Emissions of Polychlorinated Dibenzo-Dioxins and Polychlorinated Dibenzo-Furans from the Brooklyn Navy Yard Resource Recovery Facility." Prepared for the New York City Department of Sanitation, August 1984.

Harter, Philip J. "Negotiating Regulations: A Cure for Malaise." *The Georgetown Law Journal*, Vol. 17, No. 1, October 1982, pp. 1–118.

Hay, Alastain. *The Chemical Scythe: Lessons of 2,4,5-T and Dioxin* (New York: Plenum Press, 1982).

Helder, Th. "Effects of 2,3,7,8-Tetrachlorodibenzo-P-Dioxin on Early Life Stages of Two Fresh-Water Fish Species." In O. Hutzinger, R. W. Frei, E. Merian, and F. Pocchiari (eds), *Chlorinated Dioxins and Related Compounds* (New York: Pergamon Press, 1980).

Hertz, David and Howard Thomas. *Risk Analysis and Its Applications* (New York: John Wiley, 1983).

Hoel, David and Kenny Crump. "Waterborne Carcinogens: A Scientist's View." In Robert Crandall and Lester Lave (eds.), *The Scientific Basis of Health and Safety Regulation* (Washington, D.C.: The Brookings Institution, 1981).

Isensee, Allan, and Gerald Jones. "Distribution of 2,3,7,8-Tetrachlorodibenzo-p-dioxin (TCDD) in Aquatic Model Ecosystem." *Environmental Science and Technology*, Vol. 9, July 1975, pp. 668–672.

Jasanoff, Sheila. *Risk Management and Political Culture* (New York: Russell Sage Foundation, 1986).

Kasperson, Roger. "Six Propositions on Public Participation and Their Relevance for Risk Communication." *Risk Analysis*, Vol. 6, No. 3, 1986.

Kasperson, Roger, Ortwin Renn, and Paul Slovic. "The Social Amplification
    of Risk: A Conceptual Framework," CENTED, Clark University,
    Worcester, Mass., 1987.
Katz, James. "The Uses of Scientific Evidence in Congressional Policymak-
    ing: The Clinch River Breeder Reactor." *Science, Technology and
    Human Values*, Vol. 9, Issue 1, Winter 1984.
Katzenstein, Peter. *Between Power and Plenty* (Madison: University of Wis-
    consin Press, 1978).
_____. "Capitalism in One Country? Switzerland in the International Econ-
    omy." *International Organization*, Vol. 34, No. 4, 1980.
_____. *Corporatism and Change: Austria, Switzerland and the Politics of
    Industry* (Ithaca, N.Y.: Cornell University Press, 1984).
_____. "Small Nations in an Open International Economy: The Converging
    Balance of State and Society in Switzerland and Austria." In Peter
    Evans, Dietrich Rueschemeyer and Theda Skocpol (eds.), *Bringing
    the State Back In* (Cambridge: Cambridge University Press, 1985a).
_____. *Small States in World Markets* (Ithaca, N.Y.: Cornell University
    Press, 1985b).
Kelman, Steven. *Regulating America, Regulating Sweden* (Cambridge: MIT
    Press, 1981).
_____. *Making Public Policy* (New York: Basic Books, 1987).
Kendall, Sir Maurice and William Buckland. *A Dictionary of Statistical Terms*
    (London: Longman Group Ltd., 1982).
Kenega, E. E. and L. A. Norris. "Environmental Toxicity of TCDD." In
    Richard Tucker, Alvin Young, and Allen Gray (eds.), *Human and
    Environmental Risks of Chlorinated Dioxins and Related Compounds*
    (New York: Plenum Press, 1981).
Kessler, T. and J. Clark. "Saccharin, Cyclamate, and Human Bladder Can-
    cer." *Journal of the American Medical Association*, Vol. 240, 1978.
Kitschelt, Herbert. "Explaining Technology Policies: Competing Theories and
    Comparative Evidence" (draft paper), Department of Political Sci-
    ence, Duke University, February 1989.
Klapp, Merrie. "Communicating Community Risk According to Location."
    Unpublished paper, Department of Urban Studies and Planning, MIT,
    1987a.
_____. "Risk Assessment, Risk Management, and Informed Bargaining."
    Environmental Impact Assessment Review, Vol. 7, 1987b, pp. 23–35.
_____. *The Sovereign Entrepreneur: Oil Policies in Advanced and Less
    Developed Capitalist Countries* (Ithaca, N.Y.: Cornell University
    Press, 1987c).
_____. "Challenges from Smart Publics." *Environmental Professional*, Vol.
    10, No. 2, 1988.
_____. "Bargaining With Uncertainty: The Brooklyn Navy Yard Incinerator
    Dispute." *Journal of Planning Education and Research*, Vol. 8, No.
    3, 1989.

Klapp, Orrin. "Sociology and the Second Law." Unpublished manuscript, 1986.

Krasner, Stephen D. *Defending the National Interest: Raw Materials, Investments and the U.S. Foreign Policy* (Princeton, N.J.: Princeton University Press, 1978).

Krimsky, Sheldon and Alonzo Plough. *Environmental Hazards: Communicating Risks as a Social Process* (Dover, MA: Auburn House 1988).

Kuhn, Thomas. *The Structure of Scientific Revolutions* (Chicago: University of Chicago Press, 1962).

Kunreuther, Howard. "Hazard Compensation and Incentive Systems: An Economic Perspective." in National Academy of Engineering, *Hazards: Technology and Fairness*, 1986, pp. 145–163.

Kunreuther, Howard and Joanne Linnerooth. "Low Probability Accidents." *Risk Analysis*, Vol. 4, No. 2, 1984.

Kunreuther, Howard and Joanne Linnerooth et al., *Risk Analysis and Decision Processes* (Laxenburg, Austria: International Institute for Applied System Analysis, 1983).

Lave, Lester and Arthur Upton (eds.). *Toxic Chemicals, Health, and The Environment* (Baltimore: Johns Hopkins University Press, 1987).

Lecos, Chris. "Sweetness Minus Calories." *FDA Consumer*, February 1985.

Lester, Richard. "Rethinking Nuclear Power," *Scientific American*, Vol. 254, No. 3, March 1986.

Leventhal, H. "Environmental Decisionmaking and the Role of the Courts." *University of Pennsylvania Law Review*, Vol. 122, No. 3, January 1974.

Lindell, Michael and Timothy Earle. "How Close Is Close Enough: Public Perceptions of the Risks of Industrial Facilities." *Risk Analysis*, Vol. 3, No. 4, 1983.

Litai, D., D. D. Lanning, and N. C. Rasmussen. "The Public Perception of Risk." In V. T. Covello et al. (eds.), *The Analysis of Actual Versus Perceived Risks* (New York: Plenum Press, 1983).

Lowrance, William. *Of Acceptable Risk: Science and The Determination of Safety* (Los Angeles: William Kaufman, 1976).

_____. "The Nature of Risk." In Richards Schwing and Walter Albers (eds.), *Societal Risk Assessment: How Safe Is Safe Enough?* (New York: Plenum Press, 1980).

Mazur, Allan. "Disputes Between Experts." *Minerva*, Vol. XI, No. 2, April 1973.

_____. *The Dynamics of Technical Controversy* (Washington, D.C.: The Communications Press, 1981).

McCaffrey, David, *OSHA and the Politics of Health Regulation* (New York: Plenum Press, 1982).

McCubbins, Mathew and Thomas Schwartz. "Congressional Oversight Overlooked: Police Patrols versus Fire Alarms." *American Journal of Political Science*, Vol. 28, 1984.

McGarity, Thomas. "Judicial Review of Scientific Rulemaking." *Science, Technology and Human Values*, Vol. 9, Issue 1, Winter 1984.

Meehan, Richard. *The Atom and the Fault* (Cambridge: The MIT Press, 1984).

Melnick, R. Shep. *Regulation and the Courts: The Case of the Clean Air Act* (Washington, D.C.: The Brookings Institution, 1983).

Mendeloff, John. *The Dilemma of Toxic Substance Regulation* (Cambridge: MIT Press, 1988).

Milvy, Paul. "A General Guideline for Management of Risk from Carcinogens." *Risk Analysis*, Vol. 6, No. 1, 1986.

Mitnick, Barry. *The Political Economy of Regulation* (New York: Columbia University Press, 1980).

Moe, Terry. "The New Economics of Organizations." *American Journal of Political Science*, Vol. 28, 1984.

_____. "An Assessment of the Positive Theory of 'Congressional Dominance.' " *Legislative Studies Quarterly*, Vol. 12, No. 4, November 1987, pp. 475–520.

Morgan, M. Granger, Samuel Morris, Max Henrion, Deborah Amaral, and William Rish. "Technical Uncertainty in Quantitative Policy Analysis—A Sulfur Air Pollution Example." *Risk Analysis*, Vol. 4, No. 3, 1984.

Mulkay, Michael. *Science and the Sociology of Knowledge* (London: George Allen and Unwin, 1979).

National Environmental Policy Act (NEPA) of 1969.

National Research Council (NRC)/National Academy of Sciences (NAS). *Saccharin: Technical Assessment of Risks and Benefits* (Washington, D.C.: NAS, 1978).

_____. *Risk Assessment in the Federal Government: Managing the Process* (Washington, D.C.: National Academy Press, 1983).

_____. *Saccharin: Technical Assessment of Risks and Benefits* (Report 1). Committee for a Study of Food Safety Policy (Washington, D.C.: NAS, 1987).

Nelkin, Dorothy. "The Political Impact of Technical Expertise." *Social Studies of Science*, Vol. 5, 1975.

_____ (ed.). *Controversy: Politics of Technical Decisions* (Beverly Hills, Califi.: Sage Publications, 1979).

_____. *Selling Science* (San Francisco: W. H. Freeman, 1987).

Nelkin, Dorothy and Michael Pollack. "Public Participation in Technological Decisions: Reality or Grand Illusion?" *Technology Review* August/September 1979, pp. 54–64.

_____. *The Atom Besieged* (Cambridge: MIT Press, 1981).

Nisbet, R. and L. Ross. *Human Inference: Strategies and Shortcomings of Social Judgement* (Englewood Cliffs, N.J.: Prentice Hall, 1980).

Niskanen, William. "Bureaucrats and Politicians." *Journal of Law and Economics*, Vol. 18, December 1975.

Office of Technology Assessment (OTA), U.S. Congress. *Cancer Testing Technology and Saccharin* (Washington, D.C.: U.S. Government Printing Office, October 1977).

O'Hare, Michael, Lawrence Bacow, and Debra Sanderson. *Facility Siting and Public Opposition* (New York: Van Nostrand Reinhold, 1983).

O'Riordan, Timothy. "Assessing and Managing Nuclear Risk in the United Kingdom." In Roger Kasperson and Jeanne Kasperson, *Nuclear Risk Analysis in Comparative Perspective* (Boston: Allen and Unwin, 1987).

Osawa, Connie and Lawrence Susskind. "Mediating Science-Intensive Policy Disputes." *Journal of Policy Analysis and Management*, Vol. 5, No. 1, 1985.

Ott, Wayne. "Total Human Exposure." *Environmental Science Technology*, Vol. 19, No. 10, 1985.

Otway, H. J. and J. J. Cohen. "Revealed Preferences: Comments on the Starr Benefit-Risk Relationships." (Vienna: International Institute for Applied System Analysis, 1975).

Otway, Harry and Kerry Thomas. "Reflections on Risk Perceptions and Policy." *Risk Analysis*, Vol. 2, No. 2, 1982.

Perrow, Charles. *Normal Accidents* (New Haven, Conn.: Yale University Press, 1984).

Plough, Alonzo and Sheldon Krimsky. "The Emergence of Risk Communication Studies: Social and Political Context." *Science, Technology and Human Values*, Vol. 12, Issues 3 & 4, Summer/Fall 1987, pp. 4–10.

Popper, Frank. "LP/HC and LULUs: The Political Uses of Risk Analysis in Land-Use Planning." *Risk Analysis*, Vol. 3, No. 4, 1983.

Popper, Karl. *Objective Knowledge* (Oxford: The Clarendon Press, 1972).

Price, Don. *The Scientific Estate* (Cambridge, Mass.: Harvard University Press, 1965).

Priebe, Paul and George Kauffman. "Making Government Policy Under Conditions of Scientific Uncertainty: A Century of Controversy About Saccharin in Congress and the Laboratory." *Minerva*, Vol. 18, No. 4, Winter 1980.

Raiffa, Howard. *The Art and Science of Negotiation* (Cambridge: Harvard University Press, 1983).

Rappe, C. Reported in Hay, "A Dispute Over Dow Chemical's Theory of Dioxin Traces." *Nature* (London) 281, 1979, pp. 619–620.

Ravetz, Jerome. "Uncertainty, Ignorance and Policy." In Harveis Brooks and Chester L. Cooper (eds.), *Science for Public Policy* (Elmsford, N.Y.: Pergamon Press, 1987).

Ricci, Paulo and Lawrence Molton. "Regulating Cancer Risks." *Environmental Science Technology*, Vol. 19, No. 6, 1985.

Rodgers, William, Jr. "A Hard Look at *Vermont Yankee*: Environmental Law Under Close Scrutiny." *Georgetown Law Journal*, Vol. 67, 1979, pp. 205–206, 699–727.

Romer, Thomas and Howard Rosenthal. "Political Resource Allocation, Controlled Agendas, and the Status Quo." *Public Choice*, Vol. 33, No. 4, 1978.

Ross, Stephen. "The Economic Theory of Agency: The Principal's Problem." *American Economic Review*, Vol. 12, May 1973.

Roth, Alvin (ed.). *Game-Theoretic Models of Bargaining* (Cambridge: Cambridge University Press, 1985).

Rothstein, Robert. "Consensual Knowledge and International Collaboration: Some Lessons From the Commodity Negotiations." *International Organization*, Vol. 38, No. 4, Autumn 1984.

Rowe, William. *An Anatomy of Risk* (New York: John Wiley, 1977).

_____. "Methodology and Myth." In Yacov Haimes (eds.), *Risk-Benefit Analysis in Water Resources Planning and Management* (New York: Plenum Press 1981).

Ruckelshaus, William. "Risk in a Free Society," *Risk Analysis*, Vol. 4, No. 3, 1984, p. 158.

_____. "Risk, Science, and Democracy." *Issues in Science and Technology*, Vol. 1, No. 3, 1985.

Rueschemeyer, Dietrich and Peter Evans. "The State and Economic Transformation: Toward an Analysis of the Conditions Underlying Effective Intervention." In Peter Evans, Dietrich Reuschemeyer, and Theda Skocpol, *Bringing the State Back In* (Cambridge: Cambridge University Press, 1985).

Ryan, J. J., P.-Y. Lau, J. C. Pilon, and D. Lewis. "2,3,7,8-Tetrachlorodibenzo-p-dioxin and 2,3,7,8-Tetrachlorodibenzofuran Residues in Great Lakes Commercial and Sport Fish." In Gangadhar Choudhary, Lawrence Keith, and Christoffer Rappe, *Chlorinated Dioxins and Dibenzofurans in the Total Environment* (Boston: Butterworth Publishers, 1983).

Sapolsky, Harvey. *Consuming Fears* (New York: Basic Books, 1986).

Schneiderman, Marvin. "The Uncertain Risks We Run: Hazardous Materials." In Schwing and Albers (eds.), *Societal Risk Assessment*, 1980.

Schwing, Richard and Walter Albers (eds). *Societal Risk Assessment: How Safe Is Safe Enough?* (New York: Plenum Press, 1980).

Sharlin, Harold Issadore. "EDB: A Case Study in Communicating Risk." *Risk Analysis*, Vol. 6, No. 1, 1986.

Shepsle, Kenneth. *The Giant Jigsaw Puzzle: Democratic Committee Assignments in the Modern House* (Chicago: University of Chicago Press, 1978).

Shepsle, Kenneth and Barry Weingast. "Political Preferences for the Pork Barrel." *American Journal of Political Science*, Vol. 25, February 1981, pp. 96–111.

Skocpol, Theda. "Bringing the State Back In: Strategies of Analysis in Current Research." In Peter Evans, Dietrich Rueschemeyer, and Theda

Skocpol (eds.), *Bringing the State Back In* (Cambridge: Cambridge University Press 1985).

Slovic, Paul. Unpublished research report, Appendix A.2.6., Decision Research, Eugene, Oregon, 1987.

Slovic, Paul, Baruch Fischhoff, and Sara Lichtenstein. "Expressed Preferences." Decision Research Report 80-1. Eugene, Oregon, 1980.

_____. In R. W. Kates, C. Hohenemser, and J. X. Kasperson (eds.), *Perilous Progress: Managing the Hazards of Technology* (Boulder, Colo.: Westview Press, 1985), pp. 91–125.

Sobel, J. and I. Takahashi. "A Multi-stage Model of Bargaining." *Review of Economic Studies*, Vol. 50, 1983.

Spence, Michael and Richard Zeckhauser. "Insurance, Information, and Individual Action." *American Economic Review*, Vol. 61, May 1971.

Starr, Chauncy. "Social Benefit vs. Technological Risk." *Science*, Vol. 165, 1969.

_____. "Risk Management Assessment and Acceptability." *Risk Analysis*, Vol. 5, No. 2, 1985.

State Environmental Quality Review Act (SEQRA). State of New York, effective September 1, 1976.

Subcommittee on Health and Scientific Research, Committee on Human Resources, U.S. Senate. 95th Congress. Hearing on *The Banning of Saccharin in 1977*, June 7, 1977 (Washington, DC: U.S. Government Printing Office, 1977).

Subcommittee on Health and the Environment, Committee on Interstate and Foreign Commerce, U.S. House of Representatives. Hearing on *The Banning of Saccharin in 1977* (Washington, D.C.: U.S. Government Printing Office, June 27, 1977).

Susskind, Lawrence. "Incorporating Risk Assessment into Environmental Impact Assessment." Prepared for Environmental Resources Limited, January 1982.

Susskind, Lawrence. and Jeffrey Cruikshank. *Breaking the Impasse: Consensual Approaches to Resolving Public Disputes* (New York: Basic Books, 1987).

Sutton, John. "Non-Cooperative Bargaining Theory: An Introduction." *Review of Economic Studies*, Vol. 53, 1986, pp. 709–724.

Taylor, Serge. *Making Bureaucracies Think: The Environmental Impact Statement Stratgy of Adminstrative Reform* (Stanford, Calif.: Stanford University Press, 1984).

U.S. Congress. *Administrative Procedures Act 552*: Public Information, Chapter 5, 1946.

_____. *The Saccharin Study and Labeling Act of 1977*, approved November 4, enacted November 23, 1977.

U.S. Department of Health, Education and Welfare (USOHELW), Public Health Service, Division of Pathology. "Subacute and Chronic Toxicity and Carcinogenicity of Various Dose Levels of Sodium Saccharin (pp. 169–170). Final Report, 1973.

Veith, G. D., D. L. De Foe, and B.V. Bergstedt. *Journal of Fisheries Research Board of Canada*, Vol. 36, 1979.

Vesely, W. E. and D. M. Rasmuson. "Uncertainties in Nuclear Probabilistic Risk Analyses." *Risk Analysis*, Vol. 4, No. 4, 1984.

Vogel, David. *National Styles of Regulation: Environmental Policy in Great Britain and the United States* (Ithaca, N.Y.: Cornell University Press, 1986).

Weber, Max. "Science as a Vocation." Originally published in 1919, translated and republished in H. H. Gerth and C. Wright Mills (eds.), *From Max Weber* (New York: Oxford University Press, 1958).

Weinberg, Alvin. "Science and Trans-Science." *Minerva*, April 1972.

_____. "Science and Its Limits." *Issues in Science and Technology*, Vol. 2, No. 1, Fall 1985.

Weingast, Barry. "A Principal-Agent Perspective on Congressional-Bureaucratic Relations." Paper delivered at Fifth Carnegie Conference on Political Economy, Carnegie Mellon University, June 1983.

_____. "The Congressional-Bureaucratic System: A Principal-Agent Perspective." *Public Choice*, Vol. 44, No. 1, 1984.

Weingast, Barry and Mark Moran. "Bureaucratic Discretion or Congressional Control? Regulatory Policymaking by the Federal Trade Commission." *Journal of Political Economy*, Vol. 91, No. 5, 1983.

_____. "Congress and Regulatory Agency Choice." *Journal of Political Economy*, Vol. 94, 1986a.

_____. "Congress and Regulatory Agency Choice: Reply to Muris." *Journal of Political Economy*. Vol. 94, No. 4, 1986b.

Wexler, Stephen and Jack Effron. "Burden of Proof and Cause of Action." *McGill Law Journal*, Vol. 29, 1984.

Whittemore, Alice. "Facts and Values in Risk Analysis for Environmental Toxicants." *Risk Analysis*, Vol. 3, No. 1, 1983.

Wildavsky, Aaron. *Searching for Safety*. New Brunswick, N.J.: Transaction Books, 1988.

Wilson, James (ed.). *The Politics of Regulation* (New York: Basic Books, 1980).

Winterfeldt, Detlof von and Ward Edwards. "Patterns of Conflict About Risky Technologies." *Risk Analysis*, Vol. 4, No. 1, 1984.

Wisconsin Alumni Research Foundation (WARF). "Long Term Saccharin Feeding in Rats." Final Report. Madison, 1973.

Wynne, Brian. "Technology, Risk and Participation: On the Social Treatment of Uncertainty." In J. Conrad (ed.), *Society, Technology and Risk Assessment* (London: Academic Press, 1980).

_____. "Uncertainty—Technical and Social." In Harvey Brooks and Chester Cooper (eds.), *Science for Public Policy (Elmsford, N.Y.: Pergamon Press, 1987)*.

Young, Oran. *Bargaining: Formal Theories of Negotiation* (Chicago: University of Illinois Press, 1975).

LEGAL CASES

Bell v. Goddard, C.A. Ind. 1966, 366 F 2nd 177.
City of Romulus v. Wayne County, D.C. Mich. 1975, 392 F. Supp. 578.
Columbia Basin Land Protection Association v. Kleppe, D.C. Washington, 1976, 417 F. Supp. 46.
Environmental Defense Fund (Matter of) v. Flacke, 96 AD 2d 862, 465 NYS 759 (2d Dep't 1983).
Environmental Defense Fund, Inc. v. Ruckelshaus, 1971, 439 F 2nd 584, 142, U.S. App. D.C. 74.
Gulf South Insulation v. Consumer Product Safety Commission, 701 F 2nd 1137 (5th Cir., 1983).
Jackson (Matter of) v. New York State Urban Development Corporation, NY 2d, May 8, 1986.
Laws of New York, ch. 612, 88-0103, 88-0109, 1975.
Movement Against Destruction v. Trainor, D.C. Md. 1975, 400 F. Supp. 533.
Natural Resources Defense Council, Inc. v. Callaway, D.C. Conn. 1974 (F. Supp. 1263, reversed in part on grounds 524 F 2nd 79.)
Natural Resources Defense Council, Inc. v. Morton, 1972, 458 F 2nd 827, 148 U.S. App. D.C. 5.
NRDC v. EPA Court of Appeals for D.C. Circuit, No. 85-1150 (argued April 29, 1987, decided July 28, 1987).
Public Law 91-190, January 1, 1970.
Robles v. Environmental Protection Agency, C.A. Md. 1973, 484 F. 2nd 843.
Schiff, Ruth, et al. (Application of) v. Board of Estimate of the City of New York et al. Supreme Court, Kings County, November 26, 1985.
—Affidavit of Dr. Theodore Goldfarb (sworn to April 16, 1985 and annexed to petition verified April 16, 1985).
Schiff Ruth, et al. (In Matter of) v. Board of Estimate of the City of New York et al. Appellate Division, AD 2d 1587E, July 7, 1986.
Society of the Plastics Industry v. OSHA, D.C. Md, 1975.
Town of Henrietta v. Department of Environmental Conservation of NY, 1980, 76 A.D. 2nd 215, 430 N.Y.S. 2nd 440.
U.S. v. J.B. Williams Co., Inc., D.C.N.Y. 1975, 402 F. Supp. 796.
Wellford v. Hardin, D.C.D.C., 1970, 315 F. Supp. 768.

INTERVIEWS AND TESTIMONIES

The Saccharin Case

Federickson, Donald, M.D., Director, National Institutes of Health. Testimony given to Subcommittee on Health and Scientific Research, Committee on Human Resources, U.S. Congress, hearing on *The Banning of Saccharin in 1977* (Washington, D.C.: U.S. Government Printing Office, 1977).

Kennedy, Donald, M.D., Commissioner, Food and Drug Administration, Department of Health, Education and Welfare. Testimony given to Subcommittee on Health and The Environment, Committee on Interstate and Foreign Commerce, U.S. House of Representatives, U.S. Congress, hearing on *The Banning of Saccharin in 1977* (Washington, D.C.: U.S. Government Printing Office, 1977), pp. 54–55.

McCann, Joyce, Dr., Senior Fellow, American Cancer Society; University of California, Berkeley; and member of Office of Technology Assessment Scientific Panel. Testimony given to Subcommittee and Scientific Research, p. 65.

Oates, John, M.D., Professor, Department of Pharmacology, Vanderbilt University School of Medicine. Testimony given to Subcommittee on Health and Scientific Research, p. 79.

Robbins, Frederick, M.D., Dean Medical School, Case Western Reserve University. Testimony given to Subcommittee on Health and Scientific Research, p. 45.

The Dioxin Case

Pat Blackstone, CASE, March 10, 1989.

Mary Cole, citizen, March 14, 1989.

Dr. Barry Commoner, scientific consultant to UJO and representative of CBNS, August 12, 1986; March 15, 1989.

John Dereszewski, CAC Chairman, June 24, 1989.

Dr. Frischman, citizen, March 10, 1989.

Harold and Vivian Levy, citizens, March 13, 1989.

Jim Meyer, Special Assistant to the Deputy Sanitation Commissioner on Resource Recovery Plants, September 4, 1986; June 24, 1987; December 1, 1988.

Steven Romalewski, NYPIRG, March 10, 1989.

Rabbi Schnitzler, citizen, June 30, 1989.

Karen Shapiro, CBNS, March 11, 1989.

Bill and Lucy Sikes, citizens, March 14, 1989.

Rabbi Stauber, citizen, March 13, 1989.

The LNG Case

Mr. Arvelund, June 10, 1987.

Mr. Corwin, June 4, 1987.

Dr. James Fay, M.E., MIT, June 9, 1987.

Mr. McCarthy, Operations Manager at Distrigas LNG Plant, June 5, 1987; March 10, 1989.

The U.K. Nuclear Power Plant Case

Richard Davies, Analyst, Division of Science Education, Office of Technology Assessment, U.S. Congress, February 27, 1988.

Index

Abraham, Kenneth, 2, 3, 4, 97
Alternative case studies: LNG, dioxin, 6–8
Alternative interpretations, economic and political institutionalism, 112
American opposition: to licensing of herbicide, 108, 125; to siting of a nuclear power plant, 108–110, 125–127; to standard, for exposure to vinyl chloride, 110–111, 127–129

Badaracco, Joseph, 68, 110, 113, 123, 128, 129
Bargain, Bureaucratic, 2–4, 61, 64–66, 102–104
Bargain ignoring necessity, 48–50
Bargaining analysis, 1; of dioxin case, 95–99
Bargaining, extended, 60
Bargaining, neocorporatist, 112
Bargaining, state-society, 115
Bargaining theory, 61–66
Bargaining with uncertainty, 1–15
Bargains with citizens, 43–66

Bazelon, David, 2, 3, 97, 98
Brickman Ronald, 69, 113
British opposition: to licensing of herbicide, 104–105, 119–121; to siting of nuclear power plant, 105–106, 121–122
Brooks, Harvey, 42, 69, 75–76, 101
Burden of proof, 18, 75–77, 103
Bureaucratic Bargain, 2–4, 61, 64–66, 102–104
Burns, John, 36

Commoner, Barry, 13, 31–33, 36–39, 53–54, 57–59
Comparisons, national, 101–129; Europe and the United States, 104–112
Competitive institutions, government bodies as, 114
Controversy, scientific, 28; institutional settings, 29–30
Cooper, Chester, 42, 101
Cruikshank, Jeffrey, 54, 60

Decisions of legislature and court, 77–99

Dioxin case, 50–55, 88–98

Efron, Edith, 31, 75
Environmental policy, federal versus state mandates, 19

Fay, James, 40–42, 45, 47–50
Findings, comparative case, Europe and the United States, 111–112
"Fire alarm" oversight, 70
Fischhoff, Baruch, 40
Fisher, Roger, 60, 71
Food additives versus environmental policies, federal mandates, 20–21
Fudenberg, D., 2, 61, 102

Game theory, 61
Government: as bureaucrat 112; as regulator and bargainer, 101–104; as scientist 112
Graham, John, 42, 68, 102
Green, Laura, 102

Hall, Peter, 112, 115, 116
Hart, Fred (author of Hart report, John Hart Company), 24, 31–33, 36, 58, 90
Harter, Philip, 60
Hypothesis, 98

Ilgen, Thomas, 113
Institutionalism, economic, 114

Jasanoff, Sheila, 5, 69, 112, 113

Katzenstein, Peter, 112, 115, 118
Kennedy, Donald, 81–83
Kennedy, Senator Edward, 78–80, 84
Kitschelt, Herbert, 112, 116, 118
Klapp, Merrie, 56, 64, 112, 115, 118

Krasner, Steven, 115, 118

Leventhal, H., 3
LNG case, 39–40, 45–48

Mazur, Allan, 58, 84
McCann, Joyce, 34–35, 79–80
McCubbins, Mathew, 70
Meehan, Richard, 126–129
Melnick, Shep, 98
Merrill, Richard, 2, 97
Mitnick, Barry, 62
Moe, Terry, 2, 3, 62, 88, 102, 112, 114
Moran, Mark, 2, 3, 87, 112, 114
Morgan, M. Granger, 17, 42
Mulkay, Michael, 58

National case studies, in Europe and the United States, 119–129
Negotiation, 60, 61
Nelkin, Dorothy, 5, 43, 66, 112, 113
Neocorporatism, 115, 116
Nesson, Charles, 75
Niskanen, William, 3, 62, 86, 112, 114

Opposition, American: to licensing of herbicide, 108, 125; to siting of nuclear plant, 108–110, 125–127; to standard for exposure to vinyl chloride, 110–111, 127–129
Opposition, British: to licensing of herbicide, 104–105, 119–121; to siting of nuclear power plant, 105–106, 121–122
"Outside option," 70–72, 85

Pesonen, David, 109, 127
Pluralism, 112–113, 118
Pollack, Michael, 5, 43, 66, 112, 113

Power, threatened but not yet un-
    seated, 58–61
Primary case studies, 9–10
Principal-agent model, 62

Raiffa, Howard, 60
Rationale, bargaining, scientific un-
    certainty as, 111–112
Ricci, Paulo, 17
Risk assessment by agency scien-
    tists, 21; the LNG case, 27–28;
    the saccharin case, 21–24
Robbins, Frederick, 34, 79–80
Roberts, Marc, 102
Rogers, Representative Paul, 81–
    83, 85, 88
Roles of scientists in environmen-
    tal decisions, 30–32; risks, 32;
    types of scientific uncertainty,
    32–42
Romer, Thomas, 86
Rosenthal, Howard, 86
Ross, Stephen, 62
Roth, Alvin, 102

Saccharin case, 78–88
"Saccharin moratorium," 83, 87,
    88
Sapolsky, Harvey, 43
Schwartz, Thomas, 70
Schweiker, Senator Richard, 79–
    80, 84, 88
Scientific uncertainty: in the dioxin
    case, 92–95; political strategies
    for challenging, 84; as a ratio-
    nale, 4
Shepsle, Kenneth, 86, 87
Skocpol, Theda, 115, 118
Sobel-Takahashi model, 61
Spence, Michael, 62

State: as regulator, 116, 118; as
    scientist, 116
Statutory requirements to examine
    science, 18–19
Strategies for challenging scientific
    findings, 72–75
Summary, four types of scientific
    uncertainty, 42
Superseding the bureaucracy, 67–
    99
Susskind, Lawrence, 53, 60
Sutton, John, 2, 3, 61, 62, 71, 102

Tirole, J., 2, 102

Uncertain science, 17–42
Uncertainty: as a bargaining
    resource; 55–61; about cancer
    risks of saccharin, 14–15; about
    dioxin risks, 12–14; about fire
    risks LNG, 10–12
Uncertainty, scientific, 1; in dis-
    putes among government institu-
    tions, 102; as a rationale, 103
Ury, William, 60, 71

Vinyl chloride, lack of French op-
    position to exposure to, 106,
    123–124
Vogel, David, 112, 113

Weingast, Barry, 2, 3, 87, 112,
    114
Wexler, Stephen, 75
Wildavsky, Aaron, 44

Zeckhauser, Richard, 62

About the Author

MERRIE G. KLAPP is an Associate Professor with the Department of Urban Studies and Planning, Massachusetts Institute of Technology. A specialist in questions of political economy and environmental issues, her earlier works include the book *The Sovereign Entrepreneur* (1987) as well as articles in such journals as *Environmental Professional* and the *Journal of Planning Education and Research*.